T0016803

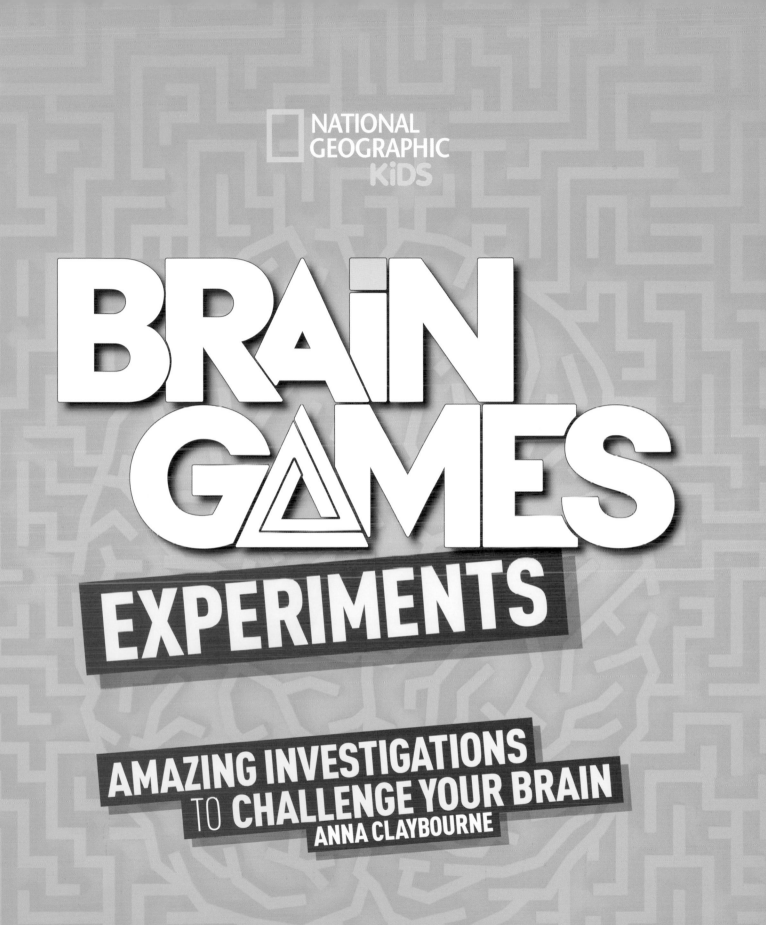

NATIONAL
GEOGRAPHIC
KiDS

BRAIN GAMES
EXPERIMENTS

AMAZING INVESTIGATIONS TO CHALLENGE YOUR BRAIN
ANNA CLAYBOURNE

NATIONAL GEOGRAPHIC
WASHINGTON, D.C.

→ CONTENTS

page 20

page 50

CHAPTER 1: BRAIN AND SENSES

CHAPTER 2: BRAIN AND BODY

page 38

page 56

CHAPTER 3: **THINKING**

CHAPTER 4: **REACTIONS**

YOU AND YOUR BRAIN

Lurking inside your head, right behind your eyeballs, is one of the most amazing things on the planet: your brain!

Humans have the most powerful, complicated brains of any species. They may look like nothing more than lumps of wrinkly gelatin, but each brain contains billions of brain cells, linked by trillions of connections, packed with vast amounts of information. These connections work in a similar way to computer circuits, making your brain one of the most complex computers ever known.

Our amazing brainpower has allowed us to develop language, invent all kinds of technology, create art, build cities, and pass on our knowledge to each other—in books like this one, for example!

→ THE BRAIN'S JOBS

The brain has so many jobs, it's impossible to list them all here.

They include tasks you are aware of, such as:

→ Making decisions about what to wear, do, read, eat, and say, as well as thousands of other things

→ Controlling your body as you move around, do tasks, or play a sport or an instrument

→ Understanding what your senses tell your brain about your surroundings

→ Remembering things you've learned, like words and numbers, facts, faces, and skills

Your brain also does other tasks in the background, without you even thinking about them:

→ Keeping your heart beating

→ Controlling your muscles so you don't fall over

→ Making you breathe, even when you're asleep

→ Sorting out which memories to store and which to delete

→ Keeping track of your body temperature, hunger, thirst, and tiredness

MEET YOUR BRAIN!

AND HERE IT IS ...

THAT WRINKLY, GELATIN-LIKE BLOB OF POWER INSIDE YOUR HEAD!

This shows what a human brain looks like from the outside—but your brain isn't blue, of course!

It's wrinkly because it has a large outer layer, called the cortex. To fit inside your skull, the cortex has to be crumpled up into lots of folds.

The cortex is actually a grayish color, and the living brain is pinkish gray because it has a lot of blood vessels running through it. These deliver the oxygen that the brain cells need in order to work.

GRAY MATTER
The cortex, or gray matter, is where we do most of our conscious thinking—the thinking that we are aware of. Different areas of the cortex deal with different things.

UNDERSTANDING SPEECH

SPEAKING

MAKING DECISIONS, CONCENTRATING, PLANNING, CALCULATING, AND CREATING

CONTROLLING MOVEMENT

TOUCHING

TASTING

HEARING

SMELLING

VISION

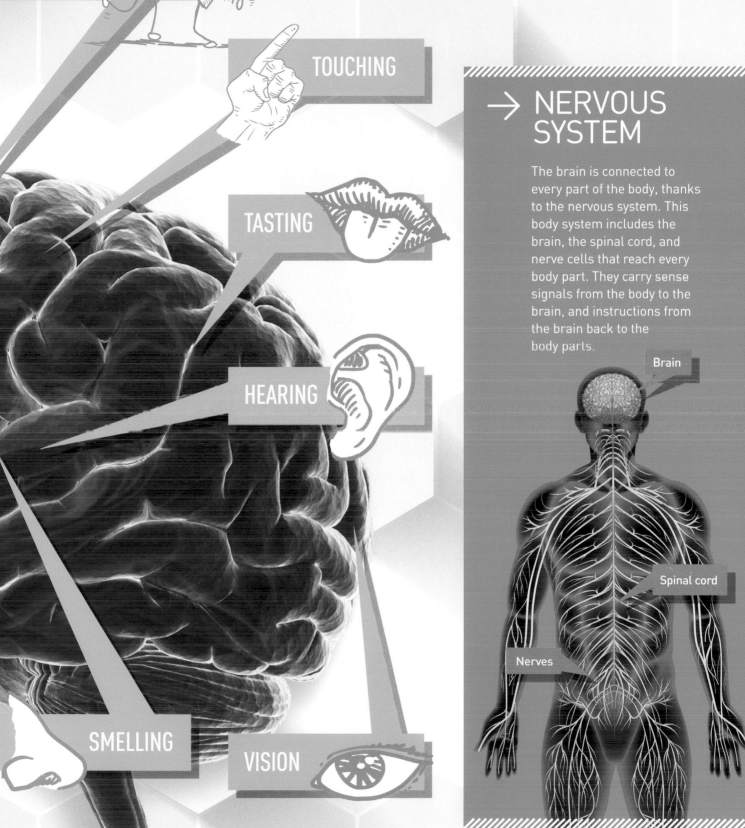

→ NERVOUS SYSTEM

The brain is connected to every part of the body, thanks to the nervous system. This body system includes the brain, the spinal cord, and nerve cells that reach every body part. They carry sense signals from the body to the brain, and instructions from the brain back to the body parts.

Brain

Spinal cord

Nerves

INSIDE THE BRAIN

Inside, the brain has several different parts and areas, which do different jobs. Here are some of them ...

YOUR BRAIN HAS AROUND 85 BILLION BRAIN CELLS ...

... WITH UP TO 100 TRILLION CONNECTIONS.

HYPOTHALAMUS
The hypothalamus helps to control your emotions, hunger, thirst, sleep, and body temperature.

BRAIN STEM
The brain stem controls basic functions such as your breathing and heartbeat.

CEREBRUM

The cerebrum is the biggest part of the brain, and is covered by the wrinkly cortex.

The cerebrum is mostly split into two separate sides, connected by the corpus callosum.

CEREBELLUM

The cerebellum, at the back of the brain, helps with moving and balancing.

SPINAL CORD

The spinal cord connects the brain to the rest of the body.

WHEN YOU'RE AWAKE, THERE'S ENOUGH **ELECTRICITY** ZAPPING AROUND YOUR BRAIN TO POWER A SMALL LIGHTBULB.

THE BRAIN IS **60% FAT!** BRAIN CELLS NEED **FAT-BASED CHEMICALS** IN ORDER TO WORK.

IT MAKES UP ABOUT **2%** OF A PERSON'S BODY WEIGHT ...

... BUT USES UP ABOUT **20%** OF THEIR ENERGY!

HOW TO USE THIS BOOK

Brain games are fun activities, games, and tests to try out on your brain, or your friends' and family's brains! They reveal all kinds of cool stuff about how the brain works, what it does without you even realizing, and what it's good at ... and NOT so good at.

You'll also find out how you can trick and confuse your brain, and how to help it do tasks more easily, too.

SAFETY GUIDELINES

→ Always ask an adult if it's OK to use household items for the activities.

→ Always conduct activities in a safe location away from cars or other people. For any activities you conduct in a public place, have an adult nearby for safety.

→ If an activity involves food or drinks, always ask an adult before anyone participates.

→ An adult should supervise any brain games that involve heat, cooking, electrical appliances, sharp tools, or blindfolds.

→ Be sure to wash your hands before and after any activity that involves food or touching other people.

→ Don't pressure anyone into taking part—people should only have their brains experimented on if they want to!

→ MAKE SMELLS DISAPPEAR!

Check out this box to see how many people you need, how long the experiment will take, and how tricky it is.

DIFFICULTY:
TIME NEEDED: 10 MINUTES
NUMBER OF PEOPLE: AT LEAST TWO

All day long, your senses send your brain a constant stream of signals. Things such as the feel of the chair you're sitting in, a bird flying by, the sound of traffic outside, the smell of a room, people cha... and millions more!

Although your brain is a super-powerful computer, it can't deal with all this information the whole time. It has to focus on whatever you're trying to think about, like playing a sports game or reading this book. So, your brain ignores information that it doesn't need. Test this out with this simple smell-sniffing brain game.

This first section will give you a bit of background detail about the experiment.

→ YOU NEED

Unsweetened cocoa powder
Ground cinnamon
A teaspoon
Three drinking cups or small bowls
Sticky notes to use as labels
A pen
A timer or stopwatch

You should be able to find everything you need for each experiment around your home.

1

WHAT'S INSIDE THE BOOK?

This book has four chapters, each containing a selection of brain games to try. Most of them don't need much equipment: just a few everyday household objects. There are outdoor and indoor brain games, and some can be done anywhere.

You don't need to work through the whole book from start to finish. You can do whichever activities you like, in any order. However, if you want to try out a brain game on a friend or family member, read through the instructions first, in case there's anything you need to set up in advance. And remember to follow our safety tips, too.

[WHAT'S GOING ON?]

WHEN YOU SNIFF ONE CUP OF POWDER FOR A FULL MINUTE, your brain realizes that it's getting the same sense signal over and over again. So it decides it doesn't need to keep taking it in and "switches off" your awareness of that signal. When you keep smelling the cocoa, for example, your brain starts to ignore the smell sensors that tell your brain "I'm getting a chocolaty cocoa smell." Then, when you smell the mixture, it's hard for you to detect the cocoa, because your brain is still ignoring that smell instead. So the same mixture smells different, and you only smell the cocoa.

It happens with other things, too, such as when there's a continuous sound. You start to ignore it, and often only remember it was there when it stops. And you don't feel your socks on your feet all day, because your brain ignores continuous touch sensations.

SEAL ISLAND IN SOUTH AFRICA IS SAID TO BE ONE OF THE WORLD'S SMELLIEST PLACES, THANKS TO ITS MIXTURE OF DEAD FISH AND SEAL POOP!

→ STEPS

1 Put two spoonfuls of cocoa powder into one cup, and two approximately equal spoonfuls of cinnamon into another. In the third cup, put one equal spoonful of each powder, and stir them together. Use sticky notes to label the cups.

2 Ask your test subject to smell the cocoa powder and the cinnamon powder to check if they can tell the difference. Set the timer for one minute. Ask your test subject to hold the cocoa powder cup up to their nose and smell it for the whole minute.

3 As soon as the minute is up, switch to the cup containing the mixture of both powders, and ask your test subject to take a sniff. What can they smell? Probably nothing but cinnamon!

4 [...]

The "What's Going On?" section explains the science behind what's happening in your brain when you do each experiment.

Follow the simple step-by-step guide to scientific success!

Each chapter has information about which parts of your brain are active in the experiments.

GET UP CLOSE / INSIDE YOUR BRAIN

HOW DOES YOUR BRAIN TAKE IN SENSE INFORMATION?

Your sense organs—your eyes, ears, nose, tongue, and skin—are part of your nervous system. They send signals to the brain along nerves, which are made of neurons, similar to brain cells. When the signals reach your brain, it uses different areas to process them and make sense of them.

CHAPTER ONE

BRAIN AND SENSES

Stop right now ... what's going on around you? What can you see, hear, feel, even smell, or taste? And how do you know you can?

It's because your brain is taking in a nonstop stream of information from your senses. Your eyes, ears, skin, nose, and mouth contain millions of sense-detecting cells that pick up information about the outside world. They send the signals to your brain, and it works out what they mean.

Of course, you use this sense information all the time, whether you're reading, making something, playing a game, eating, chatting, or even sitting around doing nothing. Your brain works incredibly hard to deal with all the incoming signals, sort them out, and make use of them. But sometimes, the signals can confuse your brain. And other times, what you sense isn't what's really there! $\rightarrow$

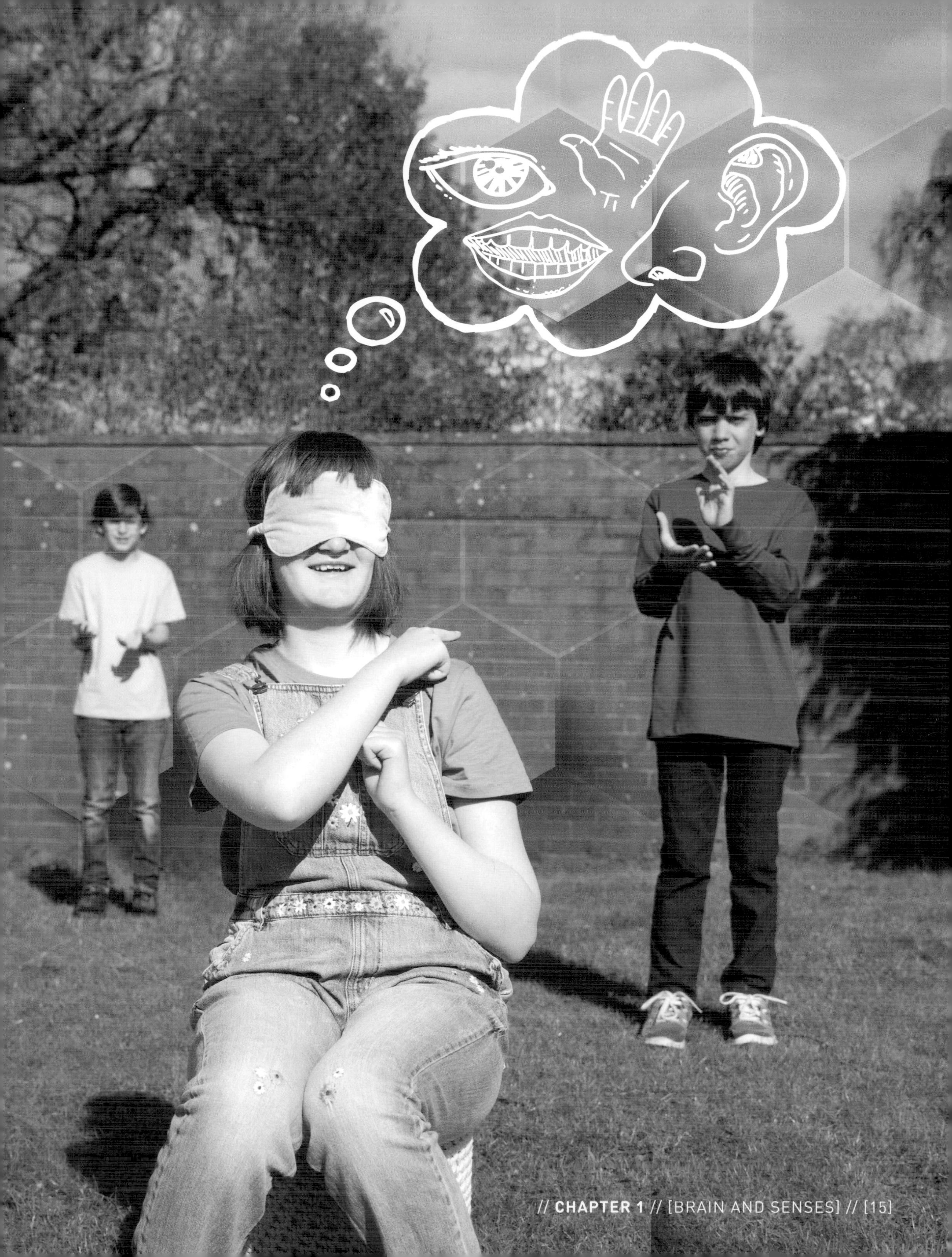

HOW DOES YOUR BRAIN TAKE IN SENSE INFORMATION?

Your sense organs—your eyes, ears, nose, tongue, and skin—are part of your nervous system. They send signals to the brain along nerves, which are made of neurons, similar to brain cells. When the signals reach your brain, it uses different areas to process them and make sense of them.

OLFACTORY CORTEX
The olfactory cortex deals with smell information.

TEMPORAL LOBES
The temporal lobes on the sides of the brain make sense of sounds and speech.

BRAIN STEM
Although other parts of the brain process sounds, it's the brain stem that calculates which ear hears a sound first and where sounds are coming from, as shown in the "Math Genius!" experiment on page 28.

SENSORY CORTEX
Touch sensations are processed in the sensory cortex.

GUSTATORY CORTEX
The gustatory cortex deals with taste information.

PARIETAL LOBE
The parietal lobe processes all the different types of sense information to give you a sense of yourself and your surroundings. It's hard at work when you do the "Real Rubber Hand" illusion on page 26.

OCCIPITAL LOBE
The occipital lobe deals with visual information from the eyes.

AMYGDALA
The amygdala controls emotions in response to sense information—such as enjoying the taste of the pink milk in the "It Tastes Pink!" experiment on page 24.

THALAMUS
Most sense signals pass through the thalamus, a small part deep inside the brain. It passes the signals on to the right areas.

→ IN PERSPECTIVE

DIFFICULTY: ☑☑☐◼◼

TIME NEEDED: 10 MINUTES

NUMBER OF PEOPLE: TWO

Is this girl only a few inches tall, or is she standing on top of a ginormous water bottle? As you can probably guess, it's neither of those!

Your brain just sees the picture that way, especially at first glance, thanks to a photographic trick. Try making your own version!

→ YOU NEED

A flat, wide-open space, like a beach, sports field, or schoolyard

An everyday object like a drink bottle, ball, or shoe

A digital camera with a screen viewer, such as a smartphone

GET CREATIVE!

A tiny person standing on top of an object is just the start! With a few more props and people, you can use this method to create all kinds of cool trick photos ... such as:

→ Tiny people sitting in someone else's hand or on someone's head
→ A tiny friend being chased by a huge dinosaur or robot (actually a normal-size toy!)
→ A bottle pouring water onto teeny people
→ A miniature person in giant shoes
→ Someone picking up a famous building or mountain, or even the moon!
→ A cup or ice-cream cone holding a cloud

→ STEPS

1 Ask your friend to stand about 60 feet (20 m) away. They can just stand still, or pose (without moving!) as if they're trying to balance on one foot.

2 Position your object on the ground in front of you, a few feet away (if it's too close, it won't be in focus). Crouch or lie down on the ground to look at it from a low angle.

3 Point your camera at the object and look at the image on the screen. Move around until the object lines up right underneath your friend's foot. Try to focus on both of them together. (On many smartphones you can tap the screen to set the focus.)

4 Take a photo from this position, so that it looks as if your friend is a tiny person standing on top of the object.

[WHAT'S GOING ON?]

THIS TYPE OF TRICK PHOTOGRAPHY IS SOMETIMES CALLED FORCED PERSPECTIVE. It works because looking at a photo is very different from looking at the real world. When you look at a real thing, such as your friend in the distance, your eyes focus on it. It looks sharp and clear, and any objects that are nearer or further away will look blurry.

To see this, focus your eyes on a faraway object, while holding your hand up in front of you. Your hand will look blurry. But if you focus on your hand instead, the faraway object will look blurry. This helps tell your brain that the two objects must be far apart. You know faraway objects look smaller, so you just see them as normal-size.

But when a smartphone takes a photo, it makes sure all the objects are pretty much in focus. When you look at the photo, your brain is fooled into seeing them as the same distance away, but with very strange sizes!

→ MAKING IT UP

DIFFICULTY: ☑☑☑☐☐

TIME NEEDED: 30 MINUTES

NUMBER OF PEOPLE: TWO

Our brains don't just take in images, like a camera. They actually change things, and sometimes even make things up! This amazing brain game proves it. First, you will find your friend's blind spot—a part of their eye that can't see anything. (We all have this blind spot in each of our eyes. We just don't notice it, as our brains hide it from us!)

Then try a second blind spot test to make their brain show them something that isn't there ...

→ YOU NEED
Cardboard or thick paper
Pens
Ruler

YOU **MIGHT** THINK THAT WHEN YOU LOOK AROUND YOU, YOU'RE SEEING THE **WORLD** EXACTLY AS IT IS. BUT THAT'S NOT THE **WHOLE** STORY!

YOU SENSE LIGHT WITH THE CELLS IN YOUR RETINA, AT THE BACK OF YOUR EYEBALL. But each retina has a gap in it, where the cells link to a big nerve leading to your brain. Normally, you never notice your blind spots—even if you're only using one eye! You can only find it with a special test. That's because your brain actually fills in the area you can't see with a copy of what's around it. In the test with a background, when the circle disappears into your blind spot, you see the background there instead—because your brain decides that's what must be there!

→ STEPS

1 First, take a piece of paper and draw two small black dots on it, about 4 inches (10 cm) apart. Make the dot on the left into an X, and the other one into a circle.

2 To find your friend's blind spot, hold the paper up about 12 inches (30 cm) from their face. Ask a friend to cover their left eye with their hand and focus their right eye on the X.

3 Ask your friend to slowly move their face toward the paper. At some point, they will notice that the black dot disappears. (It only works if they keep looking at the X.) This is because at a particular point the dot lines up with the blind spot on their retina, at the back of their eye, so they can't see it.

4 Next, make a second test on another piece of paper. Draw an X and a circle, as before. But this time, add a pattern behind them, such as a grid. Leave a square of white space around each of the two shapes.

5 Now do the blind spot test again. When the circle disappears, what happens? You should find the white space disappears, too, and gets filled in with the background pattern.

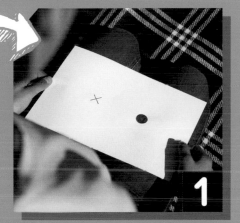

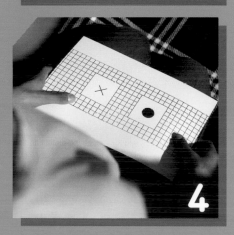

→ SIDE EYE

Most people are aware of a large, oval-shaped field of vision, reaching around the sides of their head. We feel as if we can see everything in it quite clearly, but your brain is fooling you! The edges of your field of vision are called your peripheral vision, and you actually can't see objects in this area very well at all. You probably don't think about this much, but try this brain game to test it out.

→ YOU NEED

Three colors of sturdy paper, such as index cards
Scissors

FILLING IT IN

As this experiment demonstrates, your peripheral vision actually can't see much at all, especially right at the edges. It doesn't seem that way to you, because you are constantly looking around and gathering information about what you can see. Then, your brain fills in the peripheral areas of your vision with what it already knows about the surroundings.

→ STEPS

1 First, cut six strips of paper, two of each color. Make each strip about 6 inches (15 cm) long and 1 inch (2.5 cm) wide. Cut one end of the pieces into different shapes: Make some triangle-shaped and some rounded, and leave some square.

2 Ask your friend to stand still and hold one finger up in front of them, right in the middle of their field of vision. They should focus on their finger and stay looking at it throughout the experiment.

3 Choose one of the strips of paper (without showing your friend). Tell them you're going to slowly move it into their field of vision, but they can't look directly at it—they should keep staring at their finger. They should tell you when they can first see the strip, and what color and shape it is.

4 Hold the strip up about 18 inches (45 cm) behind them with the shaped end at the top and at about eye level. Slowly walk around your friend in a circle so that you gradually move the strip into their field of vision. Where is it when they first notice it? Where is it when they can tell what shape and color it is?

5 Swap places and ask your friend to do the test on you. Did your experience differ from your friend's?

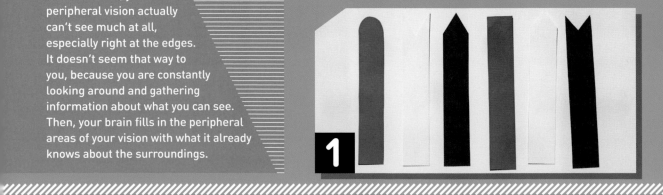

[WHAT'S GOING ON?]

MOST PEOPLE WILL SPOT THE STRIP OF PAPER ROUGHLY WHEN IT MOVES PAST THEIR EAR AND INTO THE SIDE OF THEIR FIELD OF VISION. But they may not be able to identify the color or the shape until it moves further forward. This is because signals from the edge of your field of vision hit the edge of your retina. The retina has lots of color-sensing cells, or cone cells, in the middle, but around the edges, it mainly has just rod cells, which only detect movement, light, and dark. So while your rod cells detect the presence of the card, you need to wait until your cone cells can sense it to detect the color and shape more clearly.

WHAT DO YOU SEE WHEN YOU LOOK OUT AT THE WORLD? HOW BIG IS THE AREA YOU CAN SEE— YOUR "FIELD OF VISION"? AND CAN YOU SEE EVERYTHING IN IT CLEARLY?

→ IT TASTES PINK!

Do you trust your sense of taste? If you closed your eyes and sampled a slice of lemon, some peas, or some stinky cheese, do you think you could tell the difference? You're probably thinking "Of course I could," but the way your brain experiences tastes is actually stranger than you might think. To find out more, try this brain game on friends or family.

SAFETY WARNING!

Some people are allergic to milk, lactose intolerant, or don't drink it for other reasons. They may also have allergies to ingredients in the food coloring. Check with an adult first before you or anyone else tries this game. It works just as well with soy milk, oat milk, or any other milk alternative, so ask an adult to help you choose what to use.

OVERLAPPING SENSES

Some people have synesthesia, which makes their senses seem to overlap or combine. They might hear a musical note, and experience a shade of blue. Or they might taste a food and experience a touch sensation or shape. Is this you? Scientists think as many as one in 300 people could be synesthetic.

[WHAT'S GOING ON?]

IF YOUR TEST SUBJECTS ARE LIKE MOST PEOPLE, THEY'LL PREFER THE PINK MILK, OR THINK IT TASTES BETTER—EVEN THOUGH THEY BOTH TASTE EXACTLY THE SAME. When your brain decides what a food tastes like, you're not just using your sense of taste. Your brain also uses information from your other senses, including smell, touch, and sight. For most people, sight is especially important. If you are sighted (have the ability to see), you see food before you eat it, and you start to make assumptions about it based on other foods you've tried before. You're used to pink foods, such as berries, being sweeter than green foods, such as lettuce—and this affects what you taste.

→YOU NEED

1 cup (240 mL) of milk
Two glasses
Pink food coloring
Green food coloring
Two spoons
Paper and pen

→STEPS

1 For the first step, make sure the people you want to test aren't watching. Divide the milk between the two glasses so that each glass is about half full.

2 Add a few drops of food coloring to each glass, pink in one, green in the other, and stir them in. Use enough food coloring to make the milk look obviously pink and green.

3 Now call in your first test subject, and ask them to taste the two milk drinks. Ask them what they think—do they like the drinks? How did they taste? Do they have a favorite?

4 Repeat the experiment with clean glasses for each person you want to test. Write down how people felt about the drinks. Did they like one more than the other?

THE REAL RUBBER HAND

DIFFICULTY: ☑ ☑ ☑ ☑ ☑

TIME NEEDED: 30 MINUTES

NUMBER OF PEOPLE: TWO

This experiment is designed to trick your brain into believing a rubber hand is a real part of your body—even though you know that can't be true. Unlike many optical illusions that date back a century or more, this cool brain game isn't very old. It was first discovered in the 1990s. Since then, brain scientists have invented lots more touch illusions to study how the brain works. Here's how to set up and test the rubber hand illusion on a friend, exactly the same way as the scientists did.

→ YOU NEED

A clean, dry right-handed rubber glove
Sand, cotton balls, dried lentils, beans, or rice to fill the glove
String
A table and two chairs
A large flat box, such as a pizza box, or a serving tray to use as a screen
A dish towel or other cloth
Two small paintbrushes

[WHAT'S GOING ON?]

THIS GAME IS SET UP TO CONFUSE YOUR BRAIN. Your brain is always using more than one sense at the same time. When you feel something touching you, you're getting touch signals from your skin, but you're also getting visual signals from your eyes, showing you what's causing the touch you're feeling.

Here, your brain tells you that you can feel your hand being brushed. At the same time, you can see another hand in front of you, right where your own hand should be. And it's being brushed just as your brain said your hand was.

Normally you wouldn't experience this kind of situation in real life, so your brain doesn't notice that something weird is going on. To your brain, you have a hand in front of you that's being touched by a paintbrush—which your brain can sense as it's also happening to your real hand, out of sight. And so after a while, it starts to interpret the glove as your own hand. You know it's not, of course—but that knowledge is in a different part of your brain. The result: You can "feel" your rubber hand!

→ STEPS

1 First, make your rubber right hand. Take the rubber glove and fill it with sand, cotton balls, lentils, or something similar, to make it more solid and realistic. Tie the opening of the glove closed with string.

2 Ask your test subject to sit down with their hands resting on the table. Now put the rubber right hand in front of the person, so that they can see it. Place it to match how they have their real right arm placed on the table.

3 Take the cloth and use it to cover up the tied end of the glove, like a sleeve. Drape it over the person's arm so it looks as if the rubber hand could be connected to their body.

4 Stand the cardboard box or tray on its side in between the person's right hand and the rubber hand so that they can't see their right hand.

5 Now sit opposite the person, and hold one paintbrush in each of your hands. Use the paintbrushes to gently brush the two right hands— the real one, and the rubber one. Brush them both in exactly the same way at the same time.

6 Keep doing this for a couple of minutes, while the person looks at the rubber hand. After a while, they should start to get the weird feeling that the rubber hand is their real hand, and that they can "feel" you brushing it!

7 Swap places and see if it works on you!

→ MATH GENIUS!

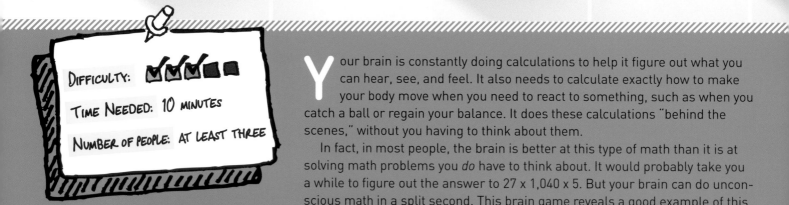

Your brain is constantly doing calculations to help it figure out what you can hear, see, and feel. It also needs to calculate exactly how to make your body move when you need to react to something, such as when you catch a ball or regain your balance. It does these calculations "behind the scenes," without you having to think about them.

In fact, in most people, the brain is better at this type of math than it is at solving math problems you *do* have to think about. It would probably take you a while to figure out the answer to 27 x 1,040 x 5. But your brain can do unconscious math in a split second. This brain game reveals a good example of this.

→YOU NEED
A blindfold
A chair

→STEPS

1 Ask one person (someone with a good sense of hearing) to be the "listener." They should put the blindfold on, making sure it doesn't cover their ears, and stand (or sit on a chair) with their back to the others.

2 The other people, the "sounders," should quietly move to different positions behind the listener, various distances to the left or right, and about 10 feet (3 m) away.

3 Once in position, the sounders should take turns clapping loudly.

4 As fast as possible after they hear the clap, the listener must point over their shoulder to where they think the sound came from. Did they get it right?

5 Next, try doing the same thing but with the sounders standing at different distances. Try doing two claps one right after another, but from different places. Finally, ask the listener to cover one ear. Can they still tell where each clap is coming from?

WHAT ELSE CAN I TRY?

HERE'S ANOTHER QUICK EXPERIMENT ...

It shows how the brain calculates how much muscle strength to use. You just need two plastic jugs, one of them filled with water. Ask a friend to hold the empty jug out and keep it as still as they can, while you steadily pour water into it from the other jug. Then, halfway through, suddenly stop pouring.

Your friend's arm will probably move upward when you stop. Why? Because their brain calculates how fast the weight of the water is increasing, and how fast to increase the muscle power to their arm to keep the jug still. When you stop suddenly, it takes a while for them to react, so their arm moves up.

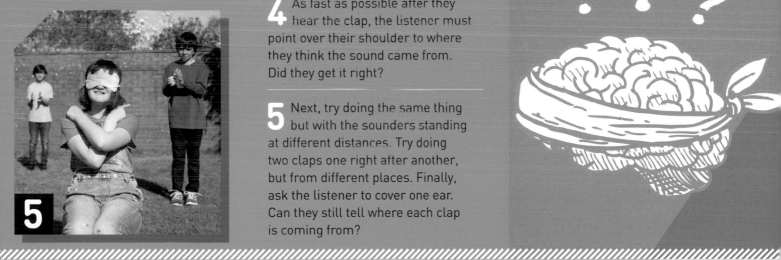

[**WHAT'S GOING ON?**] **WHEN YOU HEAR A SOUND, HOW DOES YOUR BRAIN KNOW WHERE IT'S COMING FROM?**
It might seem simple, but it can only happen because your brain uses math calculations. Your two ears are a little way apart, and each one sends its own signals to your brain when it detects a sound. If a sound is coming from one side, it will arrive at one ear a split second before the other. Your brain can sense this difference, and calculate how much sooner the first sound arrived. From this, it can figure out the angle it came from.

It's harder to calculate the direction if you only use one ear, but you can still do it. This is because the shape of your ear reflects and changes the sound. As well as comparing the signals from both ears, the brain can detect the way sound changes as it bounces around in your ears, and calculate the angle from that, too.

MAKE SMELLS DISAPPEAR!

All day long, your senses send your brain a constant stream of signals. Things such as the feel of the chair you're sitting in, a bird flying by, the sound of traffic outside, the smell of a room, people chatting—and millions more!

Although your brain is a super-powerful computer, it can't deal with all this information the whole time. It has to focus on whatever you're trying to think about, like playing a sports game or reading this book. So, your brain ignores information that it doesn't need. Test this out with this simple smell-sniffing brain game.

→ YOU NEED

Unsweetened cocoa powder
Ground cinnamon
A teaspoon
Three drinking cups or small bowls
Sticky notes to use as labels
A pen
A timer or stopwatch

WHEN YOU SNIFF ONE CUP OF POWDER FOR A FULL MINUTE, your brain realizes that it's getting the same sense signal over and over again. So it decides it doesn't need to keep taking it in and "switches off" your awareness of that signal. When you keep smelling the cocoa, for example, your brain starts to ignore the smell sensors that tell your brain "I'm getting a chocolaty cocoa smell." Then, when you smell the mixture, it's hard for you to detect the cocoa, because your brain is still ignoring that smell. Switch it around and smell cinnamon for a minute, and your brain starts ignoring that smell instead. So the same mixture smells different, and you only smell the cocoa.

It happens with other things, too, such as when there's a continuous sound. You start to ignore it, and often only remember it was there when it stops. And you don't feel your socks on your feet all day, because your brain ignores continuous touch sensations.

SEAL ISLAND IN SOUTH AFRICA IS SAID TO BE ONE OF THE WORLD'S **SMELLIEST** PLACES, THANKS TO ITS MIXTURE OF DEAD FISH AND **SEAL POOP!**

→ STEPS

1 Put two spoonfuls of cocoa powder into one cup, and two approximately equal spoonfuls of cinnamon into another. In the third cup, put one equal spoonful of each powder, and stir them together. Use sticky notes to label the cups.

2 Ask your test subject to smell the cocoa powder and the cinnamon powder to check if they can tell the difference. Set the timer for one minute. Ask your test subject to hold the cocoa powder cup up to their nose and smell it for the whole minute.

3 As soon as the minute is up, switch to the cup containing the mixture of both powders, and ask your test subject to take a sniff. What can they smell? Probably nothing but cinnamon!

4 Now repeat the experiment, but this time, your test subject needs to smell the cinnamon powder for one minute. Then switch back to the mixture, and ask them to sniff it again. What does it smell like now? This time, it's probably nothing but cocoa.

CHAPTER TWO
BRAIN AND BODY

One of your brain's most important jobs is to communicate with your body and tell it what to do. When you move your body around, your brain is in charge, even if you're not thinking about the movements you make. To control every movement, your brain has a mental map of exactly where every part of your body is in space. It also keeps track of how cold or hot your body is, where pain is coming from, and what other people's bodies are doing, too.

The brain games in this chapter reveal how the brain does these jobs—and how you can trip it up, if you know the right tricks to play! Prepare for some strange sensations. →

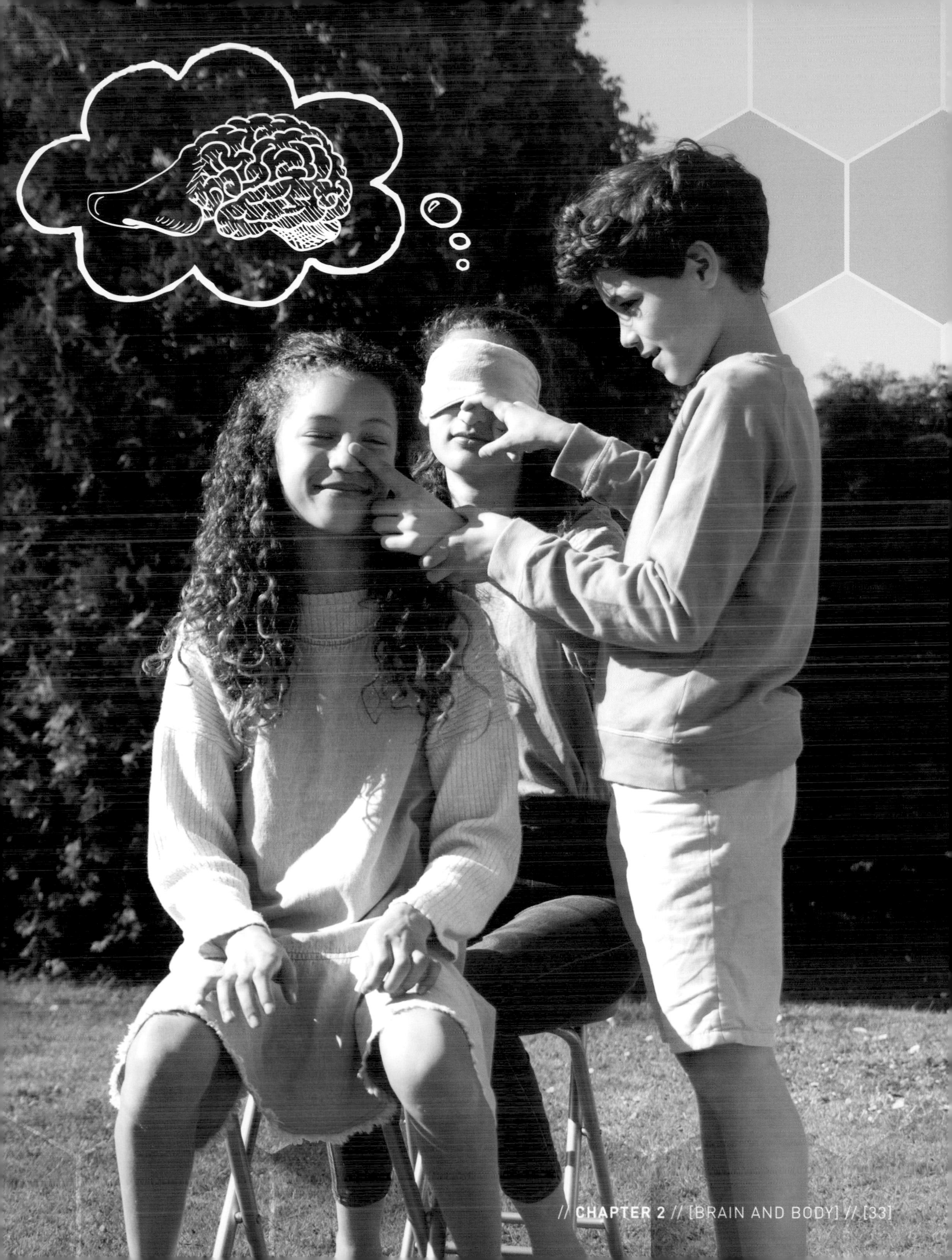

HOW THE BRAIN KEEPS TRACK OF AND CONTROLS THE BODY

While some parts of your brain are busy thinking, others work hard to keep track of what your body is experiencing, and control what it does next. Often, this happens without you thinking about it. For example, when we speak, walk, or catch a ball, we don't plan each individual movement. Instead, the brain makes the muscles work together to get things done, so that it feels automatic.

The right-hand side of your brain mainly controls the left-hand side of your body, and vice versa. The nerves cross over to the opposite side in the medulla, part of the brain stem. You can see how this works by doing "Crossover Confusion" on page 46.

MOTOR CORTEX

The motor cortex controls your body's movements.

SENSORY CORTEX

The sensory cortex deals with touch signals from all over your body.

HYPOTHALAMUS

The hypothalamus inside the brain senses temperature change signals, and regulates the body's temperature. Try out the "Weird Water" experiment on page 36 to test this.

The sensory cortex, cerebellum, and parietal cortex work together to give you your sense of proprioception, or the position your body is in. Try out "Where Am I?" on page 40 to find out about this.

PITUITARY GLAND

The pituitary gland controls many of the hormones that carry messages around the body. They control things like how you grow, digest food, and react to danger.

CEREBELLUM

The cerebellum is important for keeping your body balanced and coordinating your movements smoothly.

WEIRD WATER

DIFFICULTY: ☑☑☐☐☐

TIME NEEDED: 10 minutes

NUMBER OF PEOPLE: One kid plus an adult

Your body and your brain keep track of your temperature, so you know when to wrap up warm and when you need a cool drink. But, like so many things about the brain, it's actually not that simple. This brain game will amaze your friends, as well as your own brain!

BRRRRR, IT'S **FREEZING!** PHEW, IT'S SWELTERING! YOU KNOW WHEN IT'S **HOT** OR **COLD** ... OR **DO YOU?**

WHEN YOU PUT BOTH HANDS IN THE MIDDLE BOWL, THE WATER FEELS BOTH HOT AND COLD! The hand that's just been in the warm water feels chilly, and the hand that's been in the cold water feels warm. This is because instead of measuring the actual temperature, your brain is sensing a temperature change, as your hands cool down or heat up. The hand in the cold water had gotten used to the cold, so the warmer lukewarm water warms it up, and it feels hot—and vice versa for the hand that had been in the warm water. It's hard for you to guess the lukewarm water's exact temperature because your two hands are telling your brain different things.

→YOU NEED
Three bowls or food containers, big enough to fit your hands into
Warm and cold water from a sink or bathtub
A stopwatch or timer

→STEPS

1 Ask an adult to help you fill one of the bowls almost to the top with cold water, and another with warm water. (Not too hot—just comfortably warm, like a warm bath or shower.)

2 In the third bowl, have the adult mix an equal amount of hot and cold water to make lukewarm water. Put the three bowls on a table, with the lukewarm one in the middle.

3 With your sleeves pushed or rolled up, put one hand into the warm water and the other hand into the cold water. Leave them there for at least one minute.

4 At the end of the minute, quickly take both hands out of the bowls and put them both into the middle bowl containing lukewarm water, side by side. What does it feel like?

SPLASH! BRRRRR!
Have you noticed that a swimming pool feels cold when you first jump in, then you get used to it? This happens because your brain starts to ignore the cold signals from your skin. At the same time, it moves more blood to your internal organs to keep them warm.

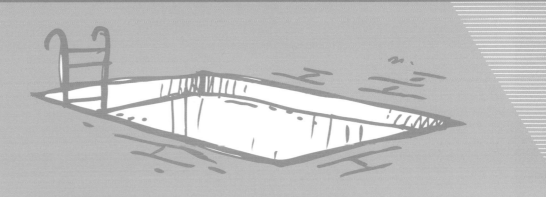

→ OLDER VS. YOUNGER

L ike other body parts, the brain grows older and changes through life, as you grow from a baby into a child, then a young adult, and then an older adult. You might think that, like some body parts, it gets weaker or more worn out as time goes on, but brains aren't quite like that ...

→ YOU NEED

People of a wide range of different ages—such as you, a parent, and a grandparent
A soft toy
A set of 10 small index cards, marked with the numbers 1 to 10
A timer or watch
Paper and pens

EXERCISE YOUR BRAIN!

Scientists have found that just like exercising your body, doing brain "exercises" like puzzles and crosswords helps people keep their brain fit and healthy.

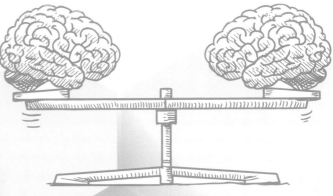

THE BRAIN IS COMPLICATED AND DOES MANY DIFFERENT TYPES OF TASKS.
Each different type of brain ability has a peak age, where you do best at that type of task. Younger people tend to do better at the reflex test, where you have to react quickly. Older people tend to do best at the word-finding test, perhaps because having lots of knowledge and experience helps with this skill. And sorting abilities usually peak somewhere in between.

1

2

3

→ STEPS

Try out these tests on different people. Use a pen and paper to keep track of everyone's score.

1 You and your test subject should stand facing each other. Hold the soft toy up so it's in front of their body and above their face. They should put their hands down by their sides. Without warning, drop the toy, and say "Left!" or "Right!" at the same moment. The person has to use that hand to try to catch the toy. Do the test 10 times, and see how many times they catch the toy with the correct hand.

2 Take the 10 index cards with numbers on them, and shuffle them into a random order. Put the pile facedown on a table in front of your test subject. Start the timer, and say "Go!" The person has to sort the cards into a row, in the right order from 1 to 10. Time how fast each person does it.

3 Give each person a pen and paper, and ask them to see how many different words they can make by rearranging the letters of the word SMART. (You can only use each letter once, but you don't have to use all five letters: e.g., ARM.) Set the timer for one minute, then count how many words each person has made.

WHERE AM I?

DIFFICULTY: ☑☐☐☐☐

TIME NEEDED: 10 MINUTES

NUMBER OF PEOPLE: AT LEAST TWO

I f you close your eyes, stick your arm out to your side, and wave it around, you still know exactly where your arm is in space. This is true even if it's not touching anything. Have you ever wondered how that can happen?

Your brain can keep track of where your body is, thanks to a sense called proprioception. There are proprioception sensors in your muscles, joints, and tendons (tough strings that link muscles to bones). They can tell when you move around and report to your brain where all your body parts are in relation to each other. But, like other brain activities, proprioception isn't always 100 percent perfect. Check out your proprioception abilities with these tests.

→ YOU NEED
Hands and fingers
An empty, safe open space with a straight line on the ground, such as a sports field

[WHAT'S GOING ON?]

AS YOU MOVE AROUND, YOUR PROPRIOCEPTION SENDS CONSTANT SIGNALS TO YOUR BRAIN ABOUT WHERE YOUR BODY IS IN ANY GIVEN SPACE. But other senses help, too—for example, your sense of sight helps you put your finger exactly on the tip of your nose as it gets closer, or put your feet on a straight line. With your eyes closed, proprioception alone isn't quite as accurate. Proprioception also works better the more you move. That's why wiggling your fingers can make it easier to find them. The more movements you make, the more signals your brain receives, so it builds up a better "map" of your body position.

→ STEPS

1 For the first test, ask your test subject to stick one hand out to their side, point their index finger, and close their eyes. Then have your test subject touch their fingertip to the tip of their nose as quickly as possible. Did they hit the tip on their first go?

2 This test's a little harder. Ask your test subject to stick one hand straight in front and diagonally up in the air, with their fingers spread out. They need to stick the other hand out to the side, also raised diagonally, and close their eyes. Keeping their first hand still, can they quickly bring the other hand over to touch the first, so that all the fingertips meet up? Not so easy!

3 Now try test two again, but this time ask your test subject to wiggle their fingers while they do the test. Does this make it easier to match the fingertips together?

4 For this test, you need an open, empty space with a straight line on the ground, such as a sports field or a paved area. Stand your test subject on a straight line with their eyes closed, and ask them to try to walk carefully along the line, placing one foot in front of the other. See how far they can get before they're off the line. You can also try this with a group of test subjects and see who can get the farthest.

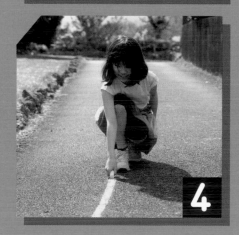

→ POWER STANCE!

DIFFICULTY: ✓✓✓☐☐

TIME NEEDED: 10 MINUTES

NUMBER OF PEOPLE: THREE

Here's your chance to do some real science research, as scientists still aren't sure about this one! Some say that standing in a "power stance" or "power pose" can make you feel stronger, braver, and more confident, and even improve your skills at some tasks. Others disagree and say it's nonsense. See if it works for you!

SOME EXPERTS THINK THAT JUST THE WAY YOU STAND CAN AFFECT YOUR BRAIN AND MAKE A **DIFFERENCE** TO HOW WELL YOU PERFORM TASKS. COULD THAT REALLY BE **TRUE?**

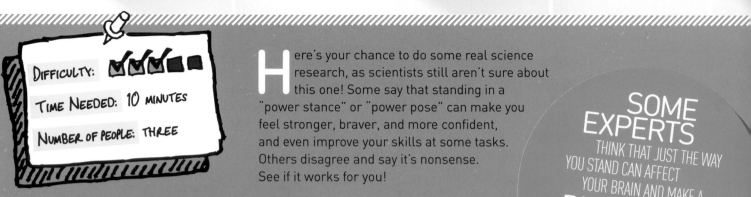

2

4

5

→ YOU NEED

A bucket or bowl
Several balls or beanbags, or
crumpled-up pieces of paper
A stopwatch or timer

→ STEPS

1 First ask one friend to practice a power pose. They will need to stand with their legs slightly apart and their hands on their hips with their elbows sticking out. Ask them to lift their chin and breathe deeply, and stay in the pose for about two minutes.

2 Ask a second friend to stand next to your first friend. The second friend should do a less powerful pose, such as hunching over or sitting down, with their arms hanging by their sides and their head hanging down, as if they're feeling tired.

3 Put a bowl or bucket about 10 feet (3 m) away from them, and put the pile of balls next to them, ready to throw.

4 After two minutes are up, ask your friends to try throwing the balls into the bowl or bucket. Give each friend 10 chances to throw, and keep score of how many they each got in.

5 Now try the experiment again, but ask your friends to swap poses. Are the results different?

MORE IDEAS

SOME OTHER ACTIVITIES TO TRY
AFTER DOING THE POSES:

See how long you can balance on one leg

See how well you can say a tongue twister

See who wins a staring contest

FUN FACT

Look at a superhero in a comic or movie, and you'll see lots of power poses! Whether or not it affects the brain, this kind of stance indicates strength and power to others.

[WHAT'S GOING ON?] DID POSING HAVE ANY EFFECT? EVEN IF IT DIDN'T CHANGE THE RESULTS, DID IT MAKE YOUR FRIENDS FEEL DIFFERENT IN ANY WAY? Scientists who support the power stance theory think that power posing can affect your brain to make you feel stronger and more confident, and could even change some of the chemicals in your body and brain, making you feel and act differently. Even if it doesn't work, though, it's possible it could have an effect on other people. Standing up tall and looking strong could make other people assume you're confident and treat you differently. What do you think?

THROUGH THE FLOOR

This brain game is easy to do, and it really messes with your mind! It makes you experience something that you definitely know isn't possible—falling through the floor, that is!—by confusing your proprioception sense. Try it on a friend first, then ask them to try it on you.

→ YOU NEED

A comfortable floor or grassy area
A timer or watch

HOW SOLID IS THE FLOOR YOU'RE STANDING ON? DO YOU THINK YOU COULD SINK RIGHT THROUGH IT? **UNLIKELY!** BUT YOU CAN MAKE YOUR BRAIN **FEEL** AS IF YOU ARE.

WHEN YOUR ARMS ARE HELD UP IN THE AIR FOR A WHILE, YOUR BRAIN STARTS IGNORING THE REPEATING SIGNALS COMING FROM THEM ABOUT WHAT POSITION YOU ARE IN—especially if you are relaxing. Eventually, your brain starts to assume that as your body is relaxed and still, you're lying on the floor already, or close to it. So, when your arms start to move down again, the only place they can be going is LOWER than the floor. Moving the arms down super slowly makes the effect stronger. Since you're moving for a long time, it feels to your brain like you must be moving a long distance.

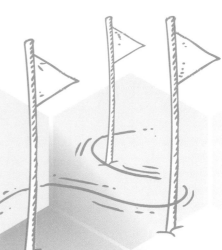

→ STEPS

1 Ask one friend to lie on the floor, facedown, with their arms stretched out in front of their head, and their eyes closed. They should relax as much as possible, and keep their eyes closed the whole time.

2 Two people should pick up your friend's hands and gently pull them up, so that their arms, head, and chest are lifted up off the floor. Hold them in this position for at least a minute.

3 Then, very slowly lower your friend's hands back down again. Their head should touch the floor first. After this, keep lowering their arms down slowly.

4 You might find your friend starts saying "Whoa! That's freaky!" or something similar, as they get the strange sensation their arms and head are falling below floor level. Swap places to experience it for yourself!

CROSSOVER CONFUSION

As you know, you have two sides—a right side and a left side—and in most people, they are roughly symmetrical. Keeping track of your left and right sides, and knowing the difference between them, is a constant task for your brain—and you can trip it up with this simple brain game.

[WHAT'S GOING ON?]

sense signals from your skin, and its awareness of right and left. When you cross your hands over, these signals don't match up. Trying to make sense of them confuses the brain, and it can get mixed up about which hands or fingers are on which side. Using spoons makes the effect even stronger, as you're not feeling the tap directly. When the spoons are double-crossed, they are back on the right sides, making the task easier again.

→YOU NEED

Two wooden spoons

→STEPS

1 Ask your friend to hold one wooden spoon in each hand, and hold them out in front of them, with their eyes closed. Now tap the two spoons with your fingers, one after the other, but very quickly so that the taps are close together. Ask your friend which spoon you tapped first, and they should get it right. Repeat the test a few times.

2 Now ask your friend to cross the wooden spoons over in front of them, and try the test again. Repeat it a few times. You'll probably find it's harder for them to tell which spoon you tapped first, and they often get it wrong.

3 Now it gets more complicated! Ask your friend to cross their arms, and then cross the spoons back over again. Repeat the test. How do they do now?

MORE IDEAS

Here's another cool crossover experiment to try. Ask your friend to hold their arms out in front of them with the palms facing outward, then cross them over so that the palms are touching. Then they should interlock their fingers and bring their hands down toward them, and then up in front of them, touching their chest.

Now point to one of their fingers, and ask them to wiggle it. Did they wiggle the correct finger?

→ PINOCCHIO'S NOSE

This baffling brain game is a little tricky to set up, but worth the effort if you can get it to work. It's related to the rubber hand illusion on page 26, but besides making you sense things differently, it also makes your brain feel as if your own body has actually changed.

WANT TO FEEL AS IF YOUR NOSE IS **INCREDIBLY** LONG? **OF COURSE YOU DO!**

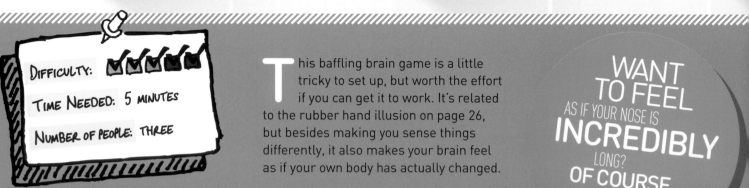

PERSON C →

PERSON A ↴

PERSON B ↓

1

2

3

→ YOU NEED

Two chairs
A blindfold

→ STEPS

This is a little complicated, so to make it as clear as possible, we'll call the three people A, B, and C.

1 First, arrange the two chairs one in front of the other, with a small gap between them. Person A (the one who's going to feel their nose grow!) should sit in the chair at the back and put on the blindfold.

2 Person B sits in the chair in front. Person C stands to the side of the chairs, in a position where they can reach both of the other people's noses.

3 Person C should move person A's hand around person B, and guide it so person A is touching person B's nose.

4 With their other hand, person C should put their own fingertip on person A's nose. Then they should carefully tap and rub both noses at the same time—person C should use their own finger to rub person A's nose and use person A's finger to rub person B's nose.

NO LUCK?

This brain game can be hard to get right, and doesn't work on everyone. But scientists have found that it works best if the pattern of taps and rubs on the noses is as random and unexpected as possible.

5 It's essential that both noses get tapped and rubbed in the exact same way, with the same pattern of movements. Keep doing it for 30 or 40 seconds, and if you're lucky, person A will start to feel like their nose is impossibly long!

[**WHAT'S GOING ON?**] LIKE SOME OF THE OTHER BRAIN GAMES IN THIS SECTION, THE WEIRD THING ABOUT THIS TRICK IS YOU KNOW IT CAN'T BE TRUE. And yet you can fool your brain into somehow believing you have a ginormous nose. Here's what happens. You feel your own nose being tapped. And at the same time, you feel your finger tapping the tip of a nose that's a couple of feet away from your face. And these taps seem to match up exactly, in a really random pattern. From your life experience, your brain knows that never happens. The only explanation must be that you're tapping your own nose. And for that to be true, your nose must be several feet long!

→ MIND CONTROL

DIFFICULTY: ✓✓✓✓✗

TIME NEEDED: 10 MINUTES

NUMBER OF PEOPLE: THREE

Do you think you can control or predict someone else's decisions, without them realizing? Sounds tricky—but you can give it a go with a simple game of Rock, Paper, Scissors. As you probably know if you've ever played it, Rock, Paper, Scissors is a game of chance. On the count of three, both players make a hand sign.

→ Paper beats rock (the paper wraps around the rock)
→ Rock beats scissors (rock blunts scissors)
→ And scissors beat paper (scissors cut paper)

If your hand sign beats the other player's, you win the round. Or if they're both the same, it's a tie. Simple, right? Or IS IT? Try these cunning tricks to see if you can sneakily influence or predict what the other person will play.

IT MIGHT FEEL AS IF A GAME LIKE ROCK, PAPER, SCISSORS IS RANDOM, BUT IT'S NOT. When people make decisions, their brains are influenced by all kinds of things, including lots of subconscious effects that they don't realize are happening. Understanding these effects can help you predict what people will do, and even influence them. Of course, it probably won't work every time—but it could give you enough of an advantage to win the game. After you've played, you could reveal your secret methods to your friends, and see who wins if they try using them, too. This is what happens at the real-life Rock, Paper, Scissors championships, which take place every year! The top players know all the tricks, so they are constantly trying to second-guess and double-bluff each other.

→YOU NEED

Pen and paper to write down the scores

→STEPS

1 Set up a game of Rock, Paper, Scissors with a friend, and ask a third person to write down who wins each round. Agree that you'll play a game with 15 rounds and see who gets the most wins.

2 Your first sneaky trick is to play paper as your opening move. Why? Because people are most likely to play rock first, as it makes them feel stronger. This is especially true if they feel rushed, so starting the game quickly could give you an extra advantage.

3 Next, try this: During the countdown, use your other hand to make the sign you want your opponent to make. So, for example, if you're playing with your right hand, subtly—that is, without calling any attention to what you're doing—make the scissors sign with your left hand down by your side. Then play rock. The other player may copy what they see, without realizing it, and play scissors.

4 If your opponent wins a round, they're more likely to do the same move again. So if they won with scissors, they are likely to play scissors again—so you should play rock next. Watch out for their wins and make use of them!

5 However, if someone has played the same move twice in a row, they'll probably play something else next. So if they play paper twice, play rock on the next go—because they probably won't play paper again.

ROBOT GAMES

If you want to LOSE at Rock, Paper, Scissors every single time, that's easy—just play the Rock Paper Scissors robot! Developed in 2012–13, it uses a camera to predict what its opponent is about to play from their subtle hand movements. Then, quick as a flash, it plays the defeating move.

CHAPTER THREE
THINKING

Your brain does a lot of other stuff besides thinking. But you're also still consciously thinking all the time, too. You need your brain to figure things out, make decisions, learn things, and remember things. Brains are brilliant at thinking—in fact, many people find it quite hard to make their brain "switch off" and think of nothing. Try it and see!

In these brain games, you can experiment with your power of thought and find out more about it. Can you remember more if you think about things differently? How can one type of thinking get in the way of another? And can thinking a particular way affect your control over your body? Turn the page to find out.

→

HOW DOES YOUR BRAIN THINK?

Your brain is made up of special brain cells called neurons. They have many tiny branches that reach out and connect to other neurons, forming a huge network. When you think, signals are zooming around in your brain, jumping from one neuron to the next along complicated pathways. And when you learn new things, the neurons make new connections!

FRONTAL CORTEX

The front of your brain—just inside your forehead—is called the frontal cortex. This is where you do thinking that you're aware of, such as calculating things, making decisions, and understanding what things mean or how they work.

PREFRONTAL CORTEX

You use the prefrontal cortex— found right at the front of the brain—to remember things you've just experienced. Turn to "Remember the Number!" on page 58 for an experiment that explores this.

When you do the "Mirror Maze" experiment on page 68, you use hand-eye coordination. The frontal cortex, parietal lobe, and cerebellum all work together to make it happen.

SENSORY CORTEX

Thinking mainly happens in the cortex, the brain's grayish, wrinkled outer layer.

WERNICKE'S AREA

This brain part makes sense of words.

OCCIPITAL LOBE

When you try to do the "Color Confusion" experiment on page 56, different parts of the brain end up struggling against each other! The occipital lobe at the back of the brain makes sense of what you can see.

LIMBIC SYSTEM

The limbic system inside your brain contains the amygdala, hippocampus, and hypothalamus. They help with things like emotions, hunger, and memory.

PRIMARY VISUAL CORTEX

This links to the center of your eye.

→ COLOR CONFUSION

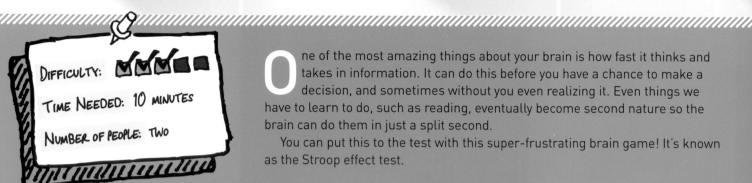

DIFFICULTY: ✓✓✓ ☐ ☐

TIME NEEDED: 10 MINUTES

NUMBER OF PEOPLE: TWO

One of the most amazing things about your brain is how fast it thinks and takes in information. It can do this before you have a chance to make a decision, and sometimes without you even realizing it. Even things we have to learn to do, such as reading, eventually become second nature so the brain can do them in just a split second.

You can put this to the test with this super-frustrating brain game! It's known as the Stroop effect test.

2

→ YOU NEED

Two large pieces of sturdy paper, at least 12 inches (30 cm) by 18 inches (45 cm)
Ruler
Pencil
Markers in red, blue, black, purple, and orange
A watch or timer

→ STEPS

1 Use your pencil and ruler to measure out and draw grids on both pieces of paper, to make a grid of 25 spaces, five spaces across and five spaces down.

2 On one grid, use your markers to write color names in the spaces on the grid, using the correct color marker for each name. For example write "BLUE" with the blue marker, "ORANGE" with the orange marker, and so on. Fill the grid with color names. It doesn't matter what order you write them in or how many times each color is used.

3 Do the same on the second grid, but this time write each color name in the wrong color. For example, write the word "BLUE" with an orange marker, the word "RED" with a black marker, and so on. Switch up what color you write each word in as you fill the grid.

4 Challenge a friend to tell you the colors of all the words on the first grid in 30 seconds. Set the timer and see if they can do it.

3

5

FUN FACT

There is one group of people who are good at the Stroop effect test, and that's younger children who haven't yet learned to read! Without their brains signaling to read the word, it's much easier for them to just see the color. If you have a younger family member or friend who hasn't learned to read yet, ask them to try it, and see if they beat you!

5 Now see if they can do it with the second grid. Try the challenge yourself, too! Remember, you have to say the color you can see, NOT what the word says. So for example, for the word BLUE written with an orange marker, you should say "orange."

[WHAT'S GOING ON?]

HOW DID YOU DO? DID YOU FIND IT A LOT HARDER TO LIST THE SECOND SET OF COLORS? Most people find that saying the colors when the words they're reading don't match takes them a lot longer, and they may also trip up and make mistakes. That's because, however hard you try, it's very hard to stop your brain from reading the words it sees. Your brain automatically recognizes the words as words—which it knows it's supposed to read—and that gets in the way of you trying to name the color of ink instead.

REMEMBER THE NUMBER!

DIFFICULTY: ☑☑☑☐☐

TIME NEEDED: 10 MINUTES

NUMBER OF PEOPLE: AT LEAST TWO

Your brain is like an enormous computer. It can do millions of calculations every second and store vast amounts of information in its memory—countless words, objects, abilities, faces, and experiences.

So it's a bit weird that it can be really hard to remember a few numbers in a row, even when you've only just looked at them. Trying to remember a sequence of just 10 numbers can be pretty tricky for most people! Test it out with this brain game.

→ YOU NEED

Pen and paper
Watch or timer

→ STEPS

1 Ask one or more friends to take a memory test. Give each person a pen and a piece of paper, and set the timer for five seconds.

2 Making sure they can't see, write a row of five numbers on another piece of paper. Show it to your friends for five seconds, then hide it and ask them to write down the numbers in the right order, from memory.

3 Do the same test again, but this time write out six numbers. Then do it with seven numbers, eight numbers, nine numbers, and 10 numbers.

4 How do your friends do? If they're like most people, they'll be able to remember up to around seven numbers fairly easily. But after that, it gets harder and they will start making mistakes.

WHY DO THINGS LIKE PHONE NUMBERS JUST FALL OUT OF YOUR **HEAD**—**AND** HOW CAN YOU GET THEM TO **STAY** THERE?

[**WHAT'S GOING ON?**] **YOU'D THINK REMEMBERING A SHORT STRING OF NUMBERS WOULD BE MUCH EASIER THAN IT IS.** The reason is that you have different types of memory! Your short-term memory stores what's happening on a moment-to-moment basis, such as where the ball is in a sports game you're watching. But it also ditches that information once it's no longer needed. Some things that happen to you, or that you learn about, get moved to your long-term memory. The more important something is to you, or the more times it's repeated, the more likely it is to get stored long-term. That's why you can remember things like words, faces, and exciting vacations.

Short-term memory can only hold a few pieces of information: up to about seven. And it tends to forget them after 20 to 30 seconds, so it can make space for other information. This is why remembering a random 10-digit number is so hard. Unless you somehow move it into your long-term memory, it will just "fall" out of your brain!

$$5:7 \quad (11+4) = 23$$
$$20-10 \quad \sqrt{\frac{1}{2}} =$$
$$-() \quad + \quad 7-1=$$
$$8:2$$
$$7 \cdot (4-2) =$$

MEMORY STORY

→

DIFFICULTY: ☑☑☑☑☐

TIME NEEDED: 30 MINUTES

NUMBER OF PEOPLE: AT LEAST THREE

THIS **BRAIN** GAME SHOWS YOU HOW TO USE A TRICK FROM THE MEMORY EXPERTS TO HELP YOU **REMEMBER** RANDOM OBJECTS.

In this brain game, instead of remembering 10 numbers, you have to remember a selection of 10 objects. Because of the way short-term memory works, it's hard to do, but there is a clever method that can turn you into a memory master!

First, try the test on friends or family members, then ask them to do it on you, and see if you can beat them using your secret skills.

→ **YOU NEED**

10 small, everyday objects
A large tray
A cloth such as a dish towel, big enough to cover the tray
Pens and paper
A watch or timer

[WHAT'S GOING ON?]

MEMORY WORKS BY LINKING OBJECTS, IDEAS, WORDS, IMAGES, AND OTHER THINGS TOGETHER IN YOUR MIND. That's why one thing often reminds you of another. It's much easier to remember things when you link them together, and give them a meaning you can relate to, such as going on vacation. Making the objects into a story links them all together and adds meaning to them—so they are much more likely to stick in your brain. There are other methods to help you remember, too. You can combine the objects into a funny picture in your head, or take their first letters of their names and use them to make a silly sentence. Believe it or not, the stranger the story, picture, or sentence is, the better it will help you remember. For example, for the objects in the main picture, you could imagine a clothesline with red (R) and yellow (Y) clothespins on it (the clothespin), and someone cutting it with scissors ... and keep going until you've built in all the objects.

→ STEPS

1 First, collect your 10 objects. Make sure they are all quite different from each other. For example, one of them could be a coin, but don't include two coins.

2 Spread the objects out on the tray, and cover them with the cloth. Ask your test subjects to come and sit in front of the tray.

3 Tell them you're going to show them 10 objects, and they have to remember as many as they can.

4 Set the timer for 30 seconds, then take off the cloth to reveal the objects. After 30 seconds, cover them up again.

5 Now give your test subjects a pen and a piece of paper to write down all the objects they can remember. How did they do? Most people only remember up to seven or eight objects.

6 Now ask someone to do the test on you. (They'll need to collect a different set of objects, of course.) Read "What's Going On?" above for a trick to help you beat their scores.

HIVE MIND

Have you ever played a guess-the-number game at a fair or party? It might be a jar full of coins or candy, or a model made from toy bricks. You have to guess how many there are in total to win a prize. It's not easy, and people usually come up with a wide range of guesses. In this brain game, you can re-create this challenge, and try a surprising method that could help you get close to the right answer.

1

→ YOU NEED

A clear glass or plastic jar (a pickle jar works well)
Lots of beads, buttons, dried beans, candy, or dried
    peas, all roughly the same size—enough to fill
    your jar
Pens and paper
A calculator

→ STEPS

1 First, fill your jar to the top with beads, buttons, or other small objects of the same kind. As in the fairground game, the aim is to have people guess how many there are.

2 Ask all the players to have a good look at the jar, guess how many objects there are inside it, and write their guess down on a piece of paper. They should guess on their own, without discussing it or looking at other people's answers.

3 Collect everyone's answers, and write them down in order from lowest to highest. Using the calculator, add all the answers together, and write the answer down. Then divide the total by the numbers of answers. So if 10 people made a guess, divide the total by 10.

4 Finally, carefully empty out your jar and count the objects inside. Is the number anywhere near the answer you came up with? Which answer was the closest?

GALTON'S OX

A famous example of the "wisdom of crowds" dates from 1906, when British scientist Francis Galton visited a country fair with a competition to guess the weight of an ox. There were 787 entries. Math-loving Galton asked to borrow the entries and study them. He discovered that the entry in the middle of the range was almost exactly right.

3

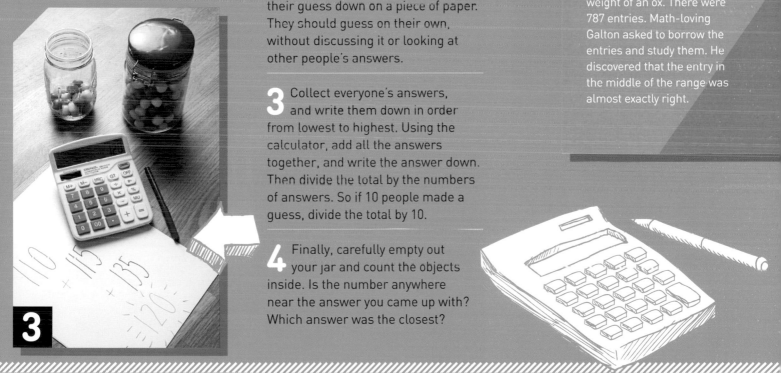

[WHAT'S GOING ON?]

IT SEEMS WEIRD THAT ADDING UP AND DIVIDING A BUNCH OF DIFFERENT GUESSES COULD GET YOU SO CLOSE TO THE REAL NUMBER, but this method—called finding the average—can actually be a really effective way of making a good guess at a number. It probably won't be exactly right, but it's likely to be in the right ballpark. It's a mathematical phenomenon known as the "wisdom of crowds," or, more modernly, the "hive mind" (like a beehive buzzing with bees).

As long as you have plenty of people (the more the better), and they make realistic guesses, the average of their guesses is usually quite close to the truth. This is because some people's answers will be roughly right, while some will be too high, and some too low. You're combining everyone's experience and guessing ability, resulting in a range of answers that hovers around the actual truth. By averaging them, you remove the too high and too low answers, and end up with a sensible guess.

→ YOU CAN DO IT!

DIFFICULTY: ✓✓✓ ■ ■

TIME NEEDED: 20 MINUTES

NUMBER OF PEOPLE: AT LEAST THREE

I f you've ever felt unsure or nervous about something, someone might have told you "You can do it!" That kind of encouragement can make you feel better. But can it actually change how well you do? Some research suggests that it can! Try out an easy encouragement experiment and see what happens.

→ YOU NEED

A square piece of cardboard about 12 inches (30 cm) on each side
Pencil
Scissors
A beanbag or soft ball (or you could use a small soft toy)
A group of several people
A blindfold

→ STEPS

1 First, you need to get several friends to agree to your plan. Read through all the steps below, and agree with your friends on what you're all going to do. Then you need to ask someone else to be the test subject—someone who doesn't know about the plan!

2 Draw a circle on the cardboard, and then draw a smaller circle inside it to make a ring. Cut the ring out and put it on the ground.

3 Tell the person being tested to stand about 10 feet (3 m) away from the cardboard ring and to try to throw the ball or toy into the middle of the ring. Keep track of how many times out of 10 tries they hit the target. Your crowd should remain silent during the trial.

4 Next, tell the person they can try again, this time wearing a blindfold. This time, your crowd should cheer, encourage them, and tell them they hit the target several times. You should then pick up the ball before their blindfold is removed.

5 Lastly, take the blindfold off and let the person have another go to see if they can beat their previous score. Again, have your crowd cheer loudly. How did the person do?

[WHAT'S GOING ON?]

THIS DOESN'T ALWAYS WORK, AND IN A REAL SCIENTIFIC EXPERIMENT YOU WOULD NEED TO TRY IT OUT WITH LOTS OF PEOPLE TO SEE HOW OFTEN IT HAD AN EFFECT. But scientists have found that in tests like this, being told you are good at something, and believing you can do it well, really can make you do better. But the opposite is true, too—if you feel like you can't do something, it often makes it harder.

The thoughts and feelings in your brain have a big influence on your body in lots of ways, and they really can affect how well you do some tasks. That's one reason why sports players often say their mental attitude is as important as their strength and skill in helping them win.

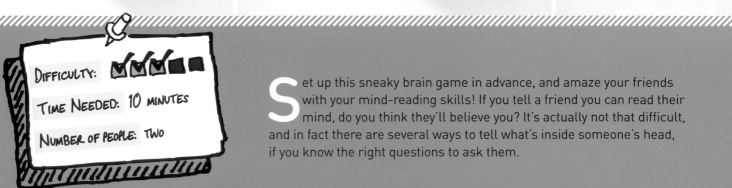

→ BE A MIND READER

Set up this sneaky brain game in advance, and amaze your friends with your mind-reading skills! If you tell a friend you can read their mind, do you think they'll believe you? It's actually not that difficult, and in fact there are several ways to tell what's inside someone's head, if you know the right questions to ask them.

→ YOU NEED

Paper
Pens

→ STEPS

1 Ahead of time, draw a carrot on a piece of paper and color it in. Or, if you'd rather not draw it, you could just write the word "Carrot." Fold up the paper and hide it near where you will be conducting the experiment—under a book or behind a cushion.

2 Once your friend is in the room, tell them that to read their mind, you first need them to do a math task. Ask them to add up all the numbers from one to five in their head, and tell you the answer. They'll think for a while, then tell you. It doesn't matter whether or not they get it right.

3 Next, ask them to do three more math problems: 1 + 5, 2 + 4, and 3 + 3. They'll probably answer 6 each time.

4 As soon as they've answered the last question, say "Now quickly tell me a vegetable!" If you're in luck, they will say "Carrot!" Why? Because almost everyone does! Open the piece of paper to show you knew what they were thinking!

MORE IDEAS

THIS TRICK WORKS WITH SEVERAL OTHER QUESTIONS, TOO. FOR EXAMPLE ...

Think of a country beginning with D ... (People usually think of Denmark.)

Think of a country beginning with F ... (People usually think of France.)

YOU CAN EVEN MIND-READ A WHOLE SEQUENCE OF ANSWERS, LIKE THIS:

Think of a country beginning with D ... (They'll probably think of Denmark.)

Think of an animal beginning with the last letter of the country you chose ... (That's a K, and they'll probably think of a kangaroo.)

Think of a fruit beginning with the last letter of the animal you chose ... (That's an O, so they'll probably think of an orange.)

[**WHAT'S GOING ON?**] THIS TRICK WORKS BECAUSE MOST PEOPLE HAVE "TYPICAL" OR "MOST OBVIOUS" EXAMPLES OF EVERYTHING STORED AWAY IN THEIR BRAINS. And for vegetables, in most Western cultures, it's usually a carrot. No one is sure why, but it could be because it's common, bright and colorful, easily recognizable, and is often seen in cartoons and children's books.

The questions you asked didn't make the person think of a carrot. In fact, you could ask any kind of question that makes the person concentrate and focus on finding the answer. The math questions distracted them and cleared their mind. So when you ask them to think of a vegetable, they don't have time to think about it—they just go for the first answer to pop into their heads. However, the trick will only work on people who are from a culture where carrots are common. If you were in a country where other vegetables are more common, you'd need a different vegetable.

→ MIRROR MAZE

DIFFICULTY: ✔✔✔☐☐

TIME NEEDED: 30 MINUTES

NUMBER OF PEOPLE: TWO

You've probably looked in the mirror loads of times, and done things like brushing your hair, cleaning your teeth, or buttoning up your coat. In this brain game, you set up a task so that you can't see your own hand, and you can only do it by looking in the mirror. It's harder than you think ... much harder!

YOU MIGHT BE USED TO DOING A FEW SIMPLE TASKS IN THE MIRROR, BUT YOU'RE NOT USED TO DOING THIS! Getting the maze right means you have to make the pen go in the right direction, and that's very difficult when you're looking at a mirror image. Your brain has learned how to make your hands move in the right directions for the real world, and it does this before you can stop it. So you'll probably find you keep going the wrong way! You have to think very hard to overcome what your brain wants your hand to do.

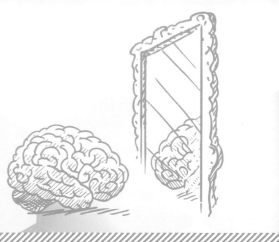

→YOU NEED

A mirror that's at least 18 inches (20 cm) wide
A chair and table
Pens and paper
A large piece of cardboard, such as the side of a packing box

→STEPS

1 First, draw a maze or find one online and print it out. Put the maze on the table, and stand the mirror behind it. If the mirror doesn't have its own stand, ask an adult to help you lean it against a wall or a stack of books, or just put the table in front of a mirror that's already fixed to the wall.

2 Sit your test subject at the desk and place the piece of cardboard in front of them so that it leans forward and blocks their view of the maze. Arrange it so that they can only see the maze by looking in the mirror.

3 Give the test subject a pen, and ask them to draw a path through the maze on the paper, while only looking at the reflection of their hand and the maze in the mirror. Is it easy? Ask them what it feels like.

MORE IDEAS

IF YOU LIKE THE MIRROR MAZE CHALLENGE, TRY THESE, TOO ...

Can you draw a star like this?

Can you draw a simple self-portrait?

Can you write your name so that it looks right in the mirror?

WHAT DOES IT LOOK LIKE?

If someone showed you a bicycle right now, you'd probably recognize it right away. You've seen thousands of them, and probably ridden one yourself. So it wouldn't be too hard to draw one, would it? For this brain game, you have to draw a bicycle—that's all! But it has to be from memory alone. Make sure you don't look at any bikes, or any pictures of bikes. Reach for the paper and give it a try.

→ YOU NEED

Paper
Pen or pencil

GET CREATIVE!

When you try to draw an object from real life, you have to look at it really carefully to take in what it actually looks like. Your brain's idea of what things like flowers, faces, and cars look like often doesn't match the reality, and can get in the way of seeing clearly. Here are some other similar things you could try drawing ...

→ The outline of a fork
→ The front door of your home
→ A horse, a dog, or another familiar animal

→ STEPS

1 Ask your test subject to sit down with a piece of paper and a pen and pencil (or just try this test for yourself). Tell them to draw a bicycle from memory, seen from the side. They don't need to draw a rider, and it doesn't have to be a brilliant drawing—just a sketch that shows the shape of a bicycle and where the main parts are.

2 Finished? Have a look at their sketch. Does it look right? Of course, if your test subject draws bicycles often and has a lot of practice, it probably will. But most people find their bicycle drawing somehow just doesn't look quite right!

3 Now show your test subject a real bicycle, or a photo of one, so they can see what they really look like.

[WHAT'S GOING ON?]

YOU MIGHT THINK YOU KNOW EXACTLY WHAT A BICYCLE LOOKS LIKE, BECAUSE YOU KNOW ONE WHEN YOU SEE IT. In fact, though, scientists think our brains don't store a full, detailed image of objects like this—unless it's something we're especially interested in for which knowing all the parts and where they are is really important to us. Instead, the brain saves memory space by only storing key details, which we can put together to recognize an object. Most people don't actually have a very good idea of what a bicycle looks like. They just know when they see one, and the details match the bits of bicycle information stored in their memory.

CHAPTER FOUR
REACTIONS

Our brains react to things all the time. If you see a coin fall out of your pocket, you react by bending down to pick it up. When your dad yells "Dinnertime!" you react by stopping what you're doing and heading for the kitchen. When you see someone you know in a crowd, you call and wave. These reactions involve conscious thinking and decision-making.

There are other types of reactions, too, though—things your brain reacts to in ways you're not aware of or can't control. Sometimes, these reactions can be helpful. Other times, they can make us get things wrong and mess up! These brain games will help you explore your reactions, and find out how they work. →

HANG ON ... WHAT JUST HAPPENED?

Your brain does billions of calculations per second. In other words, it's FAST! To run your body, keep you safe, and deal with everything that's going on around you, your brain often has to work on autopilot, because there's not enough time to think through everything you do. That's why your brain can sometimes get confused or do things you wouldn't expect.

FRONTAL CORTEX

The frontal cortex calculates how heavy you think something is going to be, so you can use the right amount of muscle power to lift it. The sensory cortex then provides feedback, telling you how heavy the object feels. Test this out on page 78 with the "Baffling Boxes" experiment.

We use a part located on the underside of the temporal lobe, known as the fusiform face area, to help us identify faces. Try the "Freaky Faces" experiment on page 88 to explore how this works.

MOTOR CORTEX

When you see a ball coming toward you and want to catch it, your frontal lobe calculates where the ball will end up. The motor cortex sends signals to the muscles to move your hand to the right place—before you can really think about it.

Inside the brain, the hippocampus and the entorhinal cortex both help you to perceive how fast time is passing, and remember when things happened. Turn to page 82 and do the "Time Testers" experiment to see how this happens.

TEMPORAL LOBE

PONS & SPINAL CORD

The pons and spinal cord handle some automatic reflexes, such as blinking when water goes in your eyes, or pulling your hand away from something hot.

FUSIFORM FACE AREA

→ CATCH IT IF YOU CAN

DIFFICULTY: ☑☑☐☐☐

TIME NEEDED: 10 MINUTES

NUMBER OF PEOPLE: AT LEAST TWO

I f someone held up a playing card, with their fingers holding the top and your hand near the bottom, and let go of it, you could catch it— couldn't you? You might be surprised to find out you probably couldn't!

Our brains are constantly reacting— taking in information from our senses, understanding it, and deciding what to do. But reacting doesn't happen instantly, even though it feels as if it does. It takes time—and in this brain game, you can find out how fast your reactions are.

→ YOU NEED

A playing card
A ruler

GET CREATIVE!

You could try testing reaction times in friends and family members of different ages—can you see a difference or a pattern? If you practice a lot, can you improve your time and get faster? Or try testing yourself at different times of day—for example:

→ When you've just woken up
→ Before and after a big meal
→ When you're about to go to sleep

→ STEPS

1 First, try the playing card experiment. Hold a card up by one end and tell a friend you're going to drop it. Your friend should try to catch it by holding their pointer finger and thumb open below the bottom end of the card.

1

2 Without warning, let go of the card so that it falls straight down. Did your friend catch it?

3 Now try the same experiment with a ruler.

4 The holder should hold the ruler at the top end, and the catcher should hold their hands apart at either side of the bottom end. When the ruler falls, they should clap their hands together to catch it.

5 If you make sure the lower numbers are at the bottom end of the ruler, the place you catch it will give you a score. The higher the score, the longer it took you to react.

5

[WHAT'S GOING ON?]

TO REACT TO A FALLING OBJECT, YOUR EYES HAVE TO SEE IT FALLING, AND SEND THAT INFORMATION TO YOUR BRAIN. Your brain has to process and make sense of it, then make a decision to try to catch it. It then has to send a signal down your arms to the right muscles. It feels as if it happens right away, but the signals take time to travel. In a healthy person, they zoom around at up to 260 miles an hour (418 km/h). That's fast—about half as fast as a plane flies. It only takes a split second for the signals to make the journey, as they're only traveling a short distance, but in that time the ruler has already fallen several inches. And if the object's a playing card, because it is shorter, it's fallen too far by the time you make the move to catch it!

BAFFLING BOXES

Most of us pick up, move, and carry various objects dozens of times each day—food and drinks, pens, books, gadgets, sports equipment, and even pets and babies! And every time, your brain has to do a calculation. It figures out how much the object probably weighs, and how much muscle power is needed to move it. That's why you don't pick up a pen and accidentally fling it into the air! Your brain is prepared for what the pen probably weighs, based on your memories and experiences.

Playing this brain game reveals what our brains are up to when we lift objects. Prepare to be surprised!

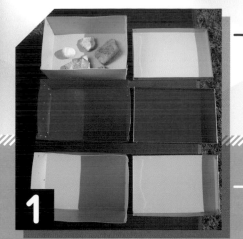

1

→ YOU NEED

Three identical boxes or containers that you can open and close. They should be opaque, not transparent, so you can't see what's inside them.
Weights such as coins or small rocks

2

3

→ STEPS

1 Ahead of time, when your test subject isn't there, put some coins or small rocks in one of the boxes as shown. Leave the other two empty, and close all the boxes.

2 Arrange the boxes in a pile on a table, with the heaviest one at the bottom. Then ask your test subject to lift up the whole stack of three boxes, and remember how heavy it feels.

3 After they put the stack down, take the bottom, heaviest box and put it on the table by itself. Now ask your test subject to pick up that box by itself, and say if it feels heavier or lighter than the stack of boxes.

4 Amazingly, when scientists do this experiment, almost everyone thinks the box on its own is heavier— even though they know that can't be possible! Did you get the same results? You could try it on several different people, and on yourself, too.

MORE IDEAS

WHAT HAPPENS IF YOU DO THE EXPERIMENT THE OTHER WAY AROUND, AND ASK THE PERSON TO LIFT THE SINGLE BOX FIRST? DOES IT STILL WORK?

[WHAT'S GOING ON?]

EVERY TIME YOU PICK SOMETHING UP, YOUR BRAIN USES WHAT IT KNOWS ABOUT IT TO ESTIMATE ITS WEIGHT FIRST. This knowledge comes from your experience, and what you can sense about the object—how it looks, what size it is, and what you think it's made of. Then the brain sends signals to your muscles to pick up that weight. With the "Baffling Boxes," you pick up the stack of three boxes first. One is much heavier than the other two, but overall, the weight is probably roughly what your brain expects. When you pick up one box, your brain decides it will probably weigh about one-third of what the stack weighs. So it sends signals to your muscles to pick up a much lighter weight. In reality, it's much heavier than your brain was expecting, and your muscles aren't prepared for it. That's why it feels really heavy!

→ STRESS TEST!

Stress is a name for feeling under pressure, overwhelmed, or in a difficult situation. You feel it in your mind, but it has an effect on your body.

Under stress, your brain tells your body to release special hormones, or body chemicals. They can help you cope, for example by giving you more energy for a while. But if you have too much stress, that can also make things harder, or even make you sick.

In this brain game, you can experiment with how stress affects getting things done—but don't worry, the stress only lasts for a short time.

→ YOU NEED

A bucket or other large container
Crumpled-up paper balls or
    Ping-Pong balls
A puzzle toy such as a jigsaw
    or Rubik's Cube
Pen and paper
A timer
Plastic bowls
    and wooden spoons

THE REASON WE FEEL STRESS IS BECAUSE IT CAN HELP US TO SURVIVE. If you're being chased by a wild animal or there's an earthquake, you need to stop what you're doing and panic, so you can get away fast. The stress-response hormones released into your body, such as adrenaline, make you better at reacting quickly and dealing with the situation.

But in other situations, stress isn't so helpful. Your brain can't help reacting to loud noises, and distractions like hearing your own name. So it takes its attention away from whatever you're trying to do. And the stress hormones in your body can make you feel jittery. That's why people under a lot of stress can become bad-tempered, clumsy, or emotional. One good solution is to have ways of relaxing and de-stressing in between stressful events or situations. Things like playing games or sports, spending time with friends or pets, reading, and being creative can all be good de-stressers.

→ STEPS

1 Ask one person to be the test subject, and give them three tasks to do:
→ Trying to throw 10 paper balls or Ping-Pong balls into a container from 10 feet (3 m) away.
→ Trying to complete or solve a puzzle toy.
→ Trying to write down the alphabet backward.

2 First, give the person one minute to spend on each task in peace and quiet, sitting somewhere comfortable, and see how well they do.

3 Then ask them to do the tasks again, but this time, make it more stressful. While they're trying to do the task, get everyone else to bang bowls with wooden spoons, and crowd around the person calling their name.

4 Observe how they manage the tasks this time around. Do they find it harder to concentrate and get the job done? Take turns and see if it's the same for everyone.

TIME TESTERS

DIFFICULTY: ✓✓✓✓☐

TIME NEEDED: 20 MINUTES

NUMBER OF PEOPLE: AT LEAST THREE

W e all deal with time every day—we know how to tell the time from a clock, and why we'll miss a bus if we don't turn up on time. But try to describe what time actually is, and it gets tricky!

Our brains have a strange relationship with time, too. It can seem to go by faster or more slowly, depending on what you're doing and what's happening around you. Try this brain game on your friends or family to see the brain's sense of time in action.

→ YOU NEED

A computer, smartphone, or other way of playing recorded music
Two pieces of music, one fast and upbeat, one much slower
A timer or watch
Pens and paper

→ STEPS

1 Tell your test subjects that you're going to test how good they are at estimating how much time is passing. Give each person a pen and a piece of paper.

2 First, play a fast, upbeat song or piece of music and ask your friends to dance to it. Using your timer or watch, keep track of how long the music is playing, and switch it off after a particular amount of time, such as 43 seconds. (Don't make it an obvious amount of time, such as one minute.)

3 Ask your test subjects to write down how many seconds they think the music lasted. Then do the same thing again, but play the slow music. Switch it off after the exact same amount of time has passed, but don't tell your subjects it's the same!

4 Lastly, do the same thing again, but with no music at all. Just let your timer run for the same amount of time, and say "Start" and "Stop" at the beginning and end.

5 Compare the results. Did people get the amount of time right? Did the fast or slow music seem to affect how much time they thought had passed?

[**WHAT'S GOING ON?**] IN EXPERIMENTS LIKE THIS, SCIENTISTS OFTEN FIND THAT FASTER MUSIC MAKES PEOPLE FEEL AS IF TIME IS GOING BY FASTER. Slower music, and silence, both make time seem slower. Did you get similar results? Your brain doesn't just detect time passing—it creates a sense of time. It takes in lots of different kinds of information from your senses, and tries to calculate how much time has passed. That means different situations affect how much time you think has gone by.

You've probably experienced this in everyday life, too. Time feels slow when you're bored and waiting for something, and keep checking the clock. It feels faster when you're distracted or in a hurry.

→ DON'T BLINK!

DIFFICULTY: ☑☑☑ ☐ ☐

TIME NEEDED: 10 MINUTES

NUMBER OF PEOPLE: AT LEAST TWO

What happens when someone tries to put a drop of eye medication in your eye, or get a speck of dirt out? It's really difficult, because however hard you try to keep your eye open, it wants to shut! This is because of your blink reflex. If anything comes near your eye or touches it even lightly, you blink. We have reflexes like this to protect us from danger and damage, such as a piece of grit flying into your eye.

But can we beat the reflex and keep our eyes open? Try this brain game to find out.

→ YOU NEED

A door with a clear glass window in it, or a ground-floor window. The window should be low enough that you can look through it when you stand on the ground outside.

Cotton balls, or small balls of crumpled-up paper

[WHAT'S GOING ON?]

A REFLEX IS AN AUTOMATIC BODY REACTION—YOU DO IT WITHOUT THINKING ABOUT IT. In fact, some reflexes don't send a signal to your brain at all! For example, if you touch a hot pan, the sense signal travels to your spine, and it immediately triggers a signal to pull your hand away. This makes you react faster, so you get less burned! A split second later, the signal reaches your brain and you understand what's happened.

The blink reflex is controlled by your brain stem, at the bottom of your brain. It works automatically, without you having to think about it. With practice, you can override the reflex and keep your eyes open. But why would you want to? We have these reflexes to keep us safe, so don't mess with success!

2

→ STEPS

1 Ask your friend to stand behind the glass door or window, with their eyes open.

2 Stand on the other side of the glass, about 6 feet (2 m) away, and throw cotton or paper balls at the person's face. Aim for their eyes!

3 Thanks to the glass, the balls cannot hit the person or hurt their eyes, and your friend knows it. But they probably still blink when the balls come near their eyes!

4 Try it again, telling your friend to try as hard as possible not to blink. Can they do it?

5 Swap places and try it yourself! How did you do?

→ SWING IT!

For hundreds of years, people have used pendulums as a kind of magical truth-finder. To do it, people would hold a pendulum still and ask it questions, such as where to find gold or maybe who they would marry. The way the pendulum swung would reveal the answer!

So what's ancient mysterious magic doing in this book? You guessed it—there's no magic here, just brain power! Try out this brain game to see it for yourself. We promise there's nothing spooky about it!

[WHAT'S GOING ON?]

MOST PEOPLE FIND THAT EVEN IF YOU TRY REALLY HARD TO HOLD THE PENDULUM TOTALLY STILL, IT SWINGS AND GIVES AN ANSWER. You can imagine how people long ago thought it was some kind of exciting magical message.

In fact, though, it's not strange at all. The person who is holding the pendulum makes it move, even if they don't realize it and don't mean to. This is called the ideomotor effect, meaning "idea-movement." If you know the answer, your brain can't help translating that into movements that make the pendulum swing the right way. This can happen subconsciously, so that you're not even aware of it happening.

In fact, even if you don't know the answer, the ideomotor effect will probably make the pendulum swing one way or the other—reflecting your best guess, or the answer you want most. So when people asked something like "Is there gold in the river?" they would still get a magical-seeming answer.

→ YOU NEED

A piece of string about 18 inches (45 cm) long
A weight, such as a key, a ring, or a large bead
Paper and pen

→ STEPS

1 First make your pendulum. Tie one end of the string to your weight, so that it can hang freely and swing around.

2 On the paper, draw two crossed lines at right angles to each other, with arrows at the ends. Mark one line "Yes" and the other one "No."

3 Ask your test subject to hold the pendulum above the crossed lines, in the middle, with the weight hanging down.

4 Explain to them that the pendulum will answer your questions by swinging in the "yes" direction or the "no" direction. They should hold it as still as possible to let it do its work.

5 Now ask the pendulum some questions about the person—ones that the test subject knows the answer to. They could be things like ...
"Does Neela like playing soccer?"
"Is Neela 11 years old?"
"Has Neela ever been to Brazil?"

6 Watch the pendulum closely as you ask each question. Does the pendulum swing in the different directions to answer the questions? Does it get the answers right?

GET CREATIVE!

To explore the ideomotor effect a little more, try doing this experiment with the person holding the pendulum blindfolded, or try asking questions they don't know the answer to. What happens then?

→ FREAKY FACES

Our brains are very good at spotting faces. As soon as we're born, we get used to looking at the faces around us and using them to identify different people. The brain is so sensitive to human faces that we even see face-like patterns in other objects, like a vending machine or a funny-looking potato.

That makes this brain game extra weird ... because it turns out that although we're great at identifying faces, we sometimes totally fail to spot unusual things about them!

[WHAT'S GOING ON?]

WHEN YOU TURN SOMEONE'S EYES AND MOUTH UPSIDE DOWN, THEY LOOK TOTALLY DIFFERENT. Yet if you look at the whole picture upside down, it doesn't look so strange—and if you know the person, you can easily recognize who it is! It's especially effective if you haven't seen the picture the right way up first. Scientists think that when you look at a face, you mainly make sense of it from its proportions—the distances between the different parts. When a face is upside down, that becomes too difficult. So the brain gives up and looks at the main features on their own instead. In isolation, they make sense, so your brain ignores the fact that you're looking at an upside-down picture! But when you see the face the right way up, your brain goes back to looking at the proportions ... and that's when you notice that something's not right!

2

3

4

➜ YOU NEED

A computer, a printer, and printer paper
Digital photos of your and your friends'
   or family's faces
Scissors
Tape or a glue stick

➜ STEPS

1 First, find or take some good photos. Each photo should show the person's face clearly, in bright lighting, looking straight at the camera.

2 Print out two copies of each photo on plain white paper. On one copy, carefully cut out neat rectangles around the eyes and mouth, making sure to keep the skin around the features intact.

3 Next, tape or glue them upside down onto the other photo.

4 Try out the illusion on a friend or family member by showing them the altered picture upside down. Do they recognize who the person is? Does the face look normal? Then flip the picture the right way up. They'll probably be amazed to see how weird it looks!

GET CREATIVE!

If you have photo-altering software and know how to use it, you could reverse the eyes and mouth on the computer first, then print the altered picture out.

Or, if you don't have a computer or printer, you can use a photo from a magazine. Look for a large picture of a face that's looking straight at the camera. Cut out the features very carefully, turn them upside down and stick them back into the same spaces.

GLOSSARY

AMYGDALA: Part of the brain that helps to control your emotions.

BRAIN STEM: A sort of "automatic control center" for several important involuntary functions of the body (things your body does automatically), including breathing, heartbeat, blood pressure, and reflexes.

CEREBELLUM: Section of the brain that deals with movement, balance, and how your muscles work together to carry out tasks.

CEREBRUM: The biggest part of the brain, split into two separate sides, called hemispheres. It controls voluntary movement (movement you actively think about, like running or jumping), speech, memory, intelligence, and emotion. It also processes sensory information from the world around you.

CONSCIOUS THINKING: When you are aware of what you are thinking and why you are thinking it. A conscious thought is something that you are actively engaged with.

CORTEX: The brain's grayish, wrinkled outer layer.

ENTORHINAL CORTEX: Together with the hippocampus, the entorhinal cortex helps you to perceive how fast time is passing and remember when things happened.

FRONTAL CORTEX: The front of your brain, just inside your forehead. It deals with conscious thinking—the thoughts that you are aware of—such as making calculations and decisions, and understanding what things mean or how they work.

FUSIFORM FACE AREA: Part of the brain that helps us identify faces.

GALTON'S OX: A mathematical idea, named after British scientist Francis Galton. He looked at all the entries in a competition to guess the weight of an ox and saw that the guess in the middle was almost exactly right. He realized that, if you have enough people, and they make realistic guesses, the average of their guesses is usually quite close to the truth.

GUSTATORY CORTEX: Part of the brain that deals with taste information.

HIPPOCAMPUS: This part of the brain plays an important role in learning and memory. It also works with the entorhinal cortex to help you to perceive how fast time is passing and remember when things happened.

HIVE MIND: A mathematical idea, also known as the "wisdom of crowds." If enough people make realistic guesses to answer a problem, the average of their guesses is usually close to the answer. By taking the average, you remove the answers that are too high and too low and end up with a sensible guess. Galton's Ox is an example of the "hive mind."

HORMONES: Chemicals that carry "messages," telling cells and body parts to do certain things. For example, hormones tell the body when to grow and when to stop growing. In humans and other animals, organs called glands release hormones into the blood so they can be carried around the body.

HYPOTHALAMUS: Part of the brain that helps to control your emotions, hunger, thirst, sleep, and body temperature.

IDEOMOTOR EFFECT: The ideomotor effect, or "idea-movement," happens when someone makes something move unconsciously, without realizing that they are doing it.

LIMBIC SYSTEM: The limbic system inside your brain is made up of the amygdala, hippocampus, and hypothalamus. They help control things such as emotions, hunger, and memory.

MEDULLA: The medulla passes messages between the spinal cord and the brain. It also helps to control breathing, digestion, the flow of blood around the body, swallowing, and sneezing.

MOTOR CORTEX: The motor cortex controls your body's movements.

NERVES: Bunches of fibers, a little like wires, that carry signals back and forth between your brain and the rest of your body.

NERVOUS SYSTEM: Your nervous system is made up of your brain, spinal cord, and all the nerves of your body. It controls everything you do, including breathing, moving, thinking, and feeling. The brain is the control center and the spinal cord is the main pathway to and from the brain. Nerves carry messages to and from the body via the spinal cord, so the brain can interpret them and take action.

NEURON: Kind of cell in the nervous system that passes information to other nerve cells, muscles, or gland cells.

OCCIPITAL LOBE: Part of the brain that processes visual information from the eyes.

OLFACTORY CORTEX: Part of the brain that processes information related to smell.

PARIETAL LOBE: This part of the brain processes all the different types of information from your senses, to help you understand your surroundings and your place in them.

PERIPHERAL VISION: The ability to see objects and movement outside of your direct line of vision—sometimes described as "out of the corner of your eye."

PITUITARY GLAND: Controls many of the hormones that carry messages around the body.

PONS: The largest part of the brain stem, connecting the cerebrum and the cerebellum, involved in many different jobs. Working together with the spinal cord, it handles some automatic reflexes, such as blinking when water goes in your eyes, or pulling your hand away from something hot.

PREFRONTAL CORTEX: You use the prefrontal cortex—found right at the front of the brain—to remember things you've just experienced.

PROPRIOCEPTION: Our sense of awareness of where our body is in space. Messages sent to the brain from sensory receptors in our muscles and joints create our sense of proprioception.

RETINA: The retina, at the back of the eye, is made up of millions of light-sensitive cells called rods and cones. When you look at something, light hits the retina, and the rods and cones send signals to the brain along the optic nerve. The brain uses these signals to work out what you are seeing.

ROD CELLS: Cells found in the retina that are very sensitive to light and allow night vision. They are concentrated at the edge of the retina, where they also enable peripheral vision.

SENSE ORGANS: The body organs that allow us to see, smell, hear, taste, and touch. The five sense organs are the eyes (seeing), nose (smelling), ears (hearing), tongue (tasting), and skin (touching).

SENSORY CORTEX: Part of the brain that processes information related to touch. It deals with touch signals from all over the body.

SPINAL CORD: A long, thin bundle of nerve fibers and tissue, enclosed in the bony spine, connecting nearly all parts of the body to the brain.

STROOP EFFECT TEST: A famous test, invented by J. Ridley Stroop in the 1930s. Participants read out a list of color words, but the words are printed in different colors—for example, the word "blue" will be colored green. The brain receives two kinds of information at once—words to read and colors to identify. This causes interference, making the task hard to do quickly.

SYNESTHESIA: A condition where someone's senses seem to overlap or combine. They might hear a musical note and experience a shade of green. Or they might taste a food and experience a touch sensation.

TEMPORAL LOBES: Parts of the brain that make sense of sounds and speech.

THALAMUS: The thalamus passes on signals to the correct areas of the brain.

WISDOM OF CROWDS: *See* Hive mind.

INDEX

MORE RESOURCES

How the Brain Works: The Facts Visually Explained. Dorling Kindersley, 2020.

Boucher Gill, Leanne. *Big Brain Book: How It Works and All Its Quirks.* Magination Press, 2021.

Drimmer, Stephanie, and Gareth Moore. *Brain Games: Big Book of Boredom Busters.* National Geographic Kids, 2018.

Drimmer, Stephanie, and Gareth Moore. *Brain Games: Colossal Book of Cranium-Crushers.* National Geographic Kids, 2020.

Drimmer, Stephanie, and Gareth Moore. *Brain Games: Mighty Book of Mind Benders.* National Geographic Kids, 2019.

Ip, Bettina. *Usborne Book of the Brain and How It Works.* Usborne, 2021.

Swanson, Jennifer. *National Geographic Kids Brain Games: The Mind-Blowing Science of Your Amazing Brain.* National Geographic Kids, 2015.

PHOTO CREDITS

ACKNOWLEDGMENTS

THANK YOU TO:

Ji-Han and Ih-Han

Alex, Henni, and Leo

Jessie, Theo, and Alex

Maisie, Henry, and Tilly

The publisher wishes to thank:
Dr. Stephen Hicks for his expert review of the content; The Dynamo, Ltd. team: Mike Atkinson, Charly Bailey, Lesley Dean, Kate Ford, Alice Humphrys, Claire Lister, Jeremy Marshall, Steve and Gill Richards, and Alicia Williamson; and the National Geographic Kids team: Shelby Lees, Brett Challos, Sarah J. Mock, Alix Inchausti, Vivian Suchman, Anne LeongSon, and Gus Tello.

Since 1888, the National Geographic Society has funded more than 14,000 research, conservation, education, and storytelling projects around the world. National Geographic Partners distributes a portion of the funds it receives from your purchase to National Geographic Society to support programs including the conservation of animals and their habitats. To learn more, visit natgeo.com/info.

For more information, visit nationalgeographic.com, call 1-877-873-6846, or write to the following address:

National Geographic Partners, LLC
1145 17th Street N.W.
Washington, DC 20036-4688 U.S.A.

For librarians and teachers: nationalgeographic.com/books/librarians-and-educators

More for kids from National Geographic:
natgeokids.com

National Geographic Kids magazine inspires children to explore their world with fun yet educational articles on animals, science, nature, and more. Using fresh storytelling and amazing photography, *Nat Geo Kids* shows kids ages 6 to 14 the fascinating truth about the world—and why they should care.
natgeo.com/subscribe

For rights or permissions inquiries, please contact National Geographic Books Subsidiary Rights: bookrights@natgeo.com

Library of Congress Cataloging-in-Publication Data

Names: Claybourne, Anna, author.
Title: Brain games : experiments / by Anna Claybourne.
Description: Washington, DC : National Geographic, 2022. | Includes index. | Audience: Ages 8-12 | Audience: Grades 4-6
Identifiers: LCCN 2021019653 | ISBN 9781426372520 (paperback) | ISBN 9781426372537 (library binding)
Subjects: LCSH: Neurosciences--Experiments--Juvenile literature. | Brain--Experiments--Juvenile literature. | Senses and sensation--Experiments--Juvenile literature.
Classification: LCC QP376 .C54 2022 | DDC 612.8--dc23
LC record available at https://lccn.loc.gov/2021019653

Printed in China
21/PPS/1